# *Imaginations*

## Dare to win the battle against your mind.

### By Jonas Clark

Unless otherwise noted, Scripture quotations are taken from the King James Version.

**Imaginations,** Dare to win the battle against your mind.

ISBN-10 1-62160-007-6
ISBN-13 978-1-62160-007-7

Copyright © 2012 by Jonas Clark

Published by Spirit of Life Publishing
A Great Commission Company
27 West Hallandale Beach Blvd.
Hallandale Beach, Florida
33009-5437, U.S.A.
(954) 456-4420

www.JonasClark.com

Printed in India

02 03 04 05 ¨ 05 04 03 02
No part of this publication may be reproduced, stored in a retrieval system, or transmitted in any form or by any means, electronic, mechanical, photocopying, scanning, or otherwise, except as permitted under Section 107 or 108 of the 1976 United States Copyright Act, without the prior written permission of the Publisher. Requests to the Publisher for permission should be addressed to the Permissions Department, Jonas Clark Ministries, 27 West Hallandale Beach Blvd., Hallandale Beach, Fla. 33009, Call 954-456-4420, e-mail:office@jonasclark.com. Jonas Clark's products are available through most bookstores. To contact Jonas Clark Ministries directly call our Customer Care Department 954-456-4420. For easy online Internet, orders visit www.jonasclark.com.

# ABOUT THE AUTHOR

Jonas Clark is first a Christian. He has authored over 55 books, written hundreds of articles and recorded thousands of audios to equip the saints and spread the gospel of the Kingdom. In 1985, Jonas Clark Ministries was founded, and later Spirit of Life Church was pioneered in Hallandale Beach, Florida, to build strong Spirit-filled believers fully trained to make a difference with their lives.

Jonas Clark Ministries is a global organization reaching the world with the exciting gospel of Jesus Christ, church planting, missions, crusades, leadership development and entrepreneurship training for senior executives, leaders, and their staff. He is a certified professional behavioral specialist with expertise with innovative research into mindsets, behaviors, emotional intelligence, skills, and relationships.

Jonas has ministered in over 32 nations, and believes all God's people are gifted to make this world a better place by establishing and advancing Christ's Word, Spirit, and Kingdom culture. Following the leading of the Holy Spirit, he founded the Apostolic Equipping Institute (with thousands of international students), the Statesmen Leadership Institute, Spirit of Life Publishing, several television and radio stations, and is president of the Global Cause Network with affiliates in the United States, Asia, and Latin America.

Jonas is an unwavering advocate of personal liberty, private property ownership, an unhampered market economy, the rule of law, constitutional guarantees of freedom of religion and the press, moral virtue, education, and international peace based on free trade.

As a husband and father, Jonas has been happily married to Rhonda for 39 years, and they have three daughters and four granddaughters. Please keep Jonas, his wife, and family in your prayers. It is God's grace on their lives and your faithful support that make it possible for the ministry to continue to be effective. For more information or invitations to speak at your next event mail to office@jonasclark.com.

" The God, who gave us life, gave us liberty at the same time."
– Thomas Jefferson

"Though we walk in the flesh, we do not war after the flesh: For the weapons of our warfare are not carnal, but mighty through God to the pulling down of strong holds; Casting down imaginations, and every high thing that exalteth itself against the knowledge of God and bringing into captivity every thought to the obedience of Christ."
(2 Corinthians 10:3-5)

# CONTENTS

Chapter 1
**THE SEEING GIFT**..................................1
Imagination is a seeing gift from God. With it, you can envision great things, dream great things and achieve great things. All outstanding achievement in life is birthed within the imagination of man.

Chapter 2
**WHISPERS IN YOUR EAR**........................21
Have you felt like you just wanted to give up and quit? Monday morning has come and you just want to ignore the alarm clock and pull the covers over your head. One of the surest signs of spiritual attack

against the mind is the feeling that you want to throw up your hands and surrender.

Chapter 3
**DEPRAVED REASONING………….………..37**
Corrupted thoughts and imaginations will battle for dominion in your mind. They war against the positive, innovative and creative ideas, dreams and aspirations the Holy Spirit wants to impart.

Chapter 4
**SATAN'S BEST WARFARE STRATEGY……53**
Satan still uses the same strategies to attack mankind, the introduction of doubt and vain imaginations. He understands that God created you to imagine all things possible, even the forbidden.

Chapter 5
**SEEING LESSONS…..…………………….…..69**
Imaginations, like all prophetic words, dreams and visions need to be judged for source, accuracy, motive, truth, purpose, intent, and clear meaning.

Chapter 6
**THE DARK GANDER…………………...……85**
Imaginations create reality, even evil reality. God

gave you freedom to choose how you respond to every circumstance in life, every thought that attacks your mind and every bad report that contradicts God's plan.

Chapter 7
**DON'T THINK LIKE THAT**......................99
How you think affects your life. Fallen man walking out of the vanity within his mind looks for ways to fulfill sensual, fleshly, lustful passions. When he finds those passions they pull on the carnal nature.

Chapter 8
**INVISIBLE OPPONENTS**..................113
Perseverance is part of the human spirit. There is not a hero in history that escaped a measure of failure before success.

Chapter 9
**WHERE DREAMS LIVE**........................129
Imaginations can change the world, your world. In fact, the world and history have already experienced change through someone's imagination. From the car you drive to the home you live in, to the clothes you wear, all have experienced the fruit of the creative power of imagination.

*Chapter 1*

# THE SEEING GIFT

*Imagination is a seeing gift from God. With it, you can envision great things, dream great things and achieve great things. All outstanding achievement in life is birthed within the imagination of man.*

Can you see yourself, sword in hand, winning the war that rages against your mind? To truly see yourself as the victorious overcomer you are, you first need to discover how God created you, a champion who is "fearfully and wonderfully made" (Psalm 139:14). God created your spirit, soul and body.

Just like God, you are a triune being. With your spirit, you connect to the unseen spirit world, with your body the natural world, and with your soul the magnificent world of imagination. Sometimes the realm of imaginations, though, can be daring. Why is that?

When you were born again, your spirit became a "new creature in Christ Jesus." Your body and soul, however, remained unchanged – and they need some serious help. Doubtless, you understand exercise and a well-balanced diet are necessary for good physical health but what about the health of your soul? It was the Apostle John that said,

> "Beloved I pray above all things that you might prosper and be in health even as your soul prospers" (3 John 1:2).

We all know a person can be born again, physically fit, and yet still suffer tremendous warfare within their mind. Struggling with that warfare is not prospering.

So how can we overcome, win this daily war in our minds, and spend our energy using our imagination the way God originally intended?

Throughout this book, you will learn proven battle tactics to help you overcome that warfare. Let's start with the soul.

## ENVISIONING GREAT THINGS

Your soul hosts your mind, will, emotions, imagination, reasoning and intellect. The warfare that attacks your mind operates within your soul, particularly your thought life and within your imagination. "So what is an imagination," you ask? An imagination is a mental vista or picture seen within the spirit of your mind. It's a picture of something created in the mind of man, or, said another way, in the spirit of man's mind. It is an image of something you see and *suppose* might happen. It is seeing yourself in a place you're not. It is a real place called the spirit of your mind, the world of the unseen within.

When God created you, He gave you the ability to "see all things as possible" within your imagination. Imagination is your seeing gift from God. With it, you can envision great things, dream great things and achieve great things. All outstanding achievement in life is birthed within the imagination of man.

Satan understands how God created you and uses your imagination and ignorance of God's Word against you. That's why it is important to "Study to show thyself approved unto God a workman that needeth not to be ashamed rightly dividing the word of truth" (2 Timothy 2:15). Before you can benefit from positive imaginations, you need to win the war against vain imaginations. Vain imaginations are those corrupted negative images and possibilities that form within the spirit of your mind when you linger on negative thoughts.

Vain imaginations defeat many believers and take them out of successful Christian living. Our imaginations, like military forts in the old American West, need to be fortified with Gospel truth. That's why Paul taught believers to renew their minds with the Word of God. The devil is a strategist. He uses imaginations to gain access into your life to steal, kill and destroy. The Apostle Paul passed on a tremendous certainty that you can use for victory. Throughout this essay, we will use it as foundational truth to help you win every battle that attacks your mind.

> "For though we walk in the flesh, we do not war after the flesh: For the weapons of our warfare are not carnal, but mighty through God to the pulling down of strong holds; Casting down imaginations, and every high thing that exalteth itself against the knowledge of God, and bringing into captivity every thought to the obedience of Christ." (2 Corinthians 10:3-5)

The Apostle Paul knew all too well that one of humanity's greatest struggles is the spiritual warfare in the mind caused by corrupted thoughts and imaginations. But from this verse in 2 Corinthians, we learn how to overcome every vain imagination and every thought that tries to take us out of the generous life Christ offers.

All men have eyes, but few can really see. It's amazing how much is written in the Bible about imagination. The realm of imagination is the realm of images. It is the place of seeing and visualizing. Scripture says, "Thou shall have no graven images (imaginations) before me" (Exodus 20:4). Our Lord never wanted His sons and daughters to worship him through graven images but with their heart and through their imaginations. With your imagination and only with your imagination can you image the greatness of God.

## WARFARE WITHIN

Consider the warfare within, and consider the spirit of your mind, the world of the unseen within. The spirit of your mind has nothing to do with your born-again spirit. The spirit of your mind is within your soul or *psuch* man (pronounced *psoo-khay*, Greek for soul). An imagination forms a mental picture of things unseen or things only seen within. Something that exists only within the imagination is a virtual world that is not real until acted on.

Again, Scripture declares, "For though we walk in the flesh we do not war after the flesh" (2 Corinthians 10:3). The warfare theme is consistent throughout the Bible. All of us are in a spiritual war for dominion. Dominion in our lives, and yes dominion within our minds. As said before, when you were saved, your spirit man was born again. You became a "new creature" in Christ Jesus (2 Corinthians 5:17). Your mind, however, didn't change. It was not born again and needs continual renewal. After salvation, you still had, for example, carnal thinking, bad information and troubling life experiences and memories that affect your judgment. Even so, God has given you mighty weapons to stop every damaging thought and corrupted imagination. With these weapons, you have authority and power to cast down every imagination and "high thing that exalts itself against the knowledge of God" in your life. He has given you the ability to bring into captivity every vain thought and imagination every time they attack your mind.

One of your greatest fighting instruments is the capacity to judge all thoughts and imaginations by the written Word of God. Unbelievers don't have this ability because their carnal minds are hostile toward God (Romans 8:7). Using the written *law of God* as your guide for truth is the first sign of spiritual maturity.

As you learn to judge all your thoughts, you will discover that fear, insecurity and confusion will leave your life.

Some have more problems with debased thoughts and imaginations than others, but there is victory for everyone. You just have to learn how to bind up ungodly thoughts and imaginations. One tactic that helps everyone is to stop considering imaginations as facts. Imaginations are only imaginations. They dwell in the unseen spirit of your mind. Thoughts, too, are only thoughts. Neither has power unless you give life to them by dwelling on them and speaking them. Life and death are in the power of the tongue, truly.

Judging every thought and imagination will help you immediately. Here's how you do it: All your thoughts and imaginations should lead you closer to God and life in the Spirit. If they don't, they are vain and corrupted and should be bound cast down and replaced with the truth

> **Imagination is your seeing gift from God. With it, you can envision great things, dream great things and achieve great things.**

of the Word of God. To embrace them hinders your walk with Christ.

## EXALTED VALLEYS

Vain imaginations never lead you closer to God but away from Him. They are exalted valleys. Many live, not according to the Word of God or the ways of God, but according to blemished imagery within their imagination. The imagination is the area where the devil works the most in the life of a believer. Just remember "the weapons of your warfare are not carnal but mighty through God to the pulling down of strongholds." Strongholds are those destructive imaginations created by dwelling on corrupted thoughts.

Imaginations will talk to you. They have a voice and are ready and willing to mentor you. Vain imaginations can, and will, laud themselves against the knowledge of God in your life if you give them an audience. They have an anti-Christ voice and challenge Christ's truth for your life. An imagination, for example, may speak to you saying, "You're going to die," when Christ's Word clearly declares, "With long life will I satisfy you and show you my salvation" (Psalm 91:16). That is just one example of how imaginations glorify themselves against the knowledge of God.

Have you ever felt defeated in the midst of victory? An imagination may also attack the Word of God in your life by saying, "You're going to be a defeated person all your life." When the Word of God says, "Blessed be the God and Father of our Lord Jesus Christ, who hath blessed us with all spiritual blessings in heavenly places in Christ" (Ephesians 1:3). When the Word of God declares, "My God shall supply all of your need according to His riches in glory by Christ Jesus" (Philippians 4:19), an imagination may attack to undermine God's plan and purpose in your life. God may speak to you saying, "I've called you for such a time as this" (Ester 4:14), but an imagination may challenge, "Yeah, but nobody loves you, nobody cares about you, and nobody will listen to you." All of these are simple examples of the lying voice of vain thoughts that attack the mind. If you stop and think about it for a moment, you can probably think of many imaginations the devil sends your way. You must learn how to get control over your thoughts and imaginations, and you can!

## IMAGINARY CONVERSATIONS

Within your imagination, you can create supposed conversations with others. Sometimes people allow imaginary verbal exchanges to lead them into error. Some start foreseeing in their mind's eye, for illustration, a presumed dialogue they'll have with someone. They may think of someone they're going to meet at work and begin to think about a discussion that has not yet taken place. Their mind begins to drift into the realm of imagination and they think about what they are going to say. They even visualize the person's response. As they continue to think about the scene, a voice of fear may be released into their imagination producing insecurity, alarm, rejection, unbelief or anger. Because imaginations produce emotion, they then find themselves envisaging things that haven't even happened. This is the poisoned fruit of corrupted thoughts and imaginations. This is why we must take every vagabond imagination captive. This realm can rob abundant life from you. Vain imaginations are "high things that exalt themselves against the knowledge of God" and attack your mind.

Have you drifted past coral reefs into the dark blue depths of a vain imagination today? You may have started thinking what your spouse *might* say, what your employer *might* say, or how your children *might* act. Suddenly your mind is consumed with unseen images that affect you in a negative way. When you dwell on corrupted thoughts you're walking, not after the Spirit, but after the flesh and you were seduced onto that path by the vain imagination. This is another example of how some live as they harvest imaginations and lose the victory of the knowledge of Christ in their lives.

Imaginations speak a foreign language and exalt themselves against the truth of God in your life. It is the voice of an imagination, for example, that says, "You can't make it. Why don't you just give up and quit?" When you hear unfamiliar sounds turn away and incline your ear towards heaven that declares, "I can do all things through Christ which strengtheneth me," (Philippians 4:13).

## PULLING DOWN PICTURES

God knows you can wander into the stormy sea of vain imaginations and quickly find yourself drowning in fear, rejection or some other assignment from the enemy. He provided in His Word, however, ways to calm every storm. Again, He says the weapons of *your* warfare are not carnal but mighty through Him to pull down those corrupted thoughts that would rise against His Word and ways in your life.

Pulling down negative thoughts is something that you have to do for yourself. It's like taking down and replacing old pictures of loved ones. Others can't do that for you. "So how often do you pull those thoughts down," you ask? Every time you have one. God will not take those thoughts captive for you. You have to do it. "How do you pull down a corrupted thought or imagination," you inquire? You pull them down by first recognizing that you have one.

You need to be able to see the imagination coming alive within your soul. *Imaginations are pictures within your mind of thoughts, events or conversations that are only in the unseen world within you.* They are not real. The devil offers you corrupted thoughts hoping you will take the bait and image them as possible and then bring them to life and fulfill his agenda.

Rogue imaginations encourage you to do things you shouldn't by releasing fear or playing on rejection. We cannot be driven by dread, insecurity or wandering minds. You *can* have the abundant life that Christ said you could have. Scripture says, "And having a readiness to revenge all disobedience when your obedience is fulfilled" (2 Corinthians 10:6). To "revenge disobedience" means stopping carnal imaginations that are noncompliant to the Word of God. Notice the Word tells you to be ready to cast them down through obedience because imaginations have no power over those that obey "the law of the Spirit of life in Christ Jesus."

When vain imaginations blather on, they always conflict with God's Word. As we explored earlier, that's how you know if your imagination is good or bad. When a thought conflicts with the Word of God you must submit yourself to God's Word and not the imagination. You can always seek safety by running into Christ's covering and away from corrupted thoughts and imaginations.

## LIVING WITH THIEVES

Many Christians are influenced by carnal imaginations. Vain imaginations are thieves. Don't live with them. You never know what family treasure they will pluck from your cupboards. When you linger on one of these fleshly thoughts, the triumph of God's Word is stolen from you. Don't flake out and wander into vain imaginations. Take hold of your mind. Like traversing a minefield, there is danger when walking out a corrupted imagination.

This bears repeating because it is so vital to your life. When you form, in the spirit of your mind, a picture or an image of something that *might* happen and act on that image you give sunshine to it. Acting on an imagination moves your life in that direction. To guard yourself you must not ponder on the thought. If you act out the thought you cross the threshold of safety and leave the path of life abundant.

Every one of us has done this. We've been manipulated, influenced and controlled by corrupted imaginations or by something we thought would happen that wasn't even real until we made it real.

There are truths that God speaks into our lives that are genuine and there are other thoughts the spirit of this world speaks that are not real. Most of the images that randomly come into your mind are vain imaginations. You can, however, like the wooden rudder on a mighty ship, direct your imaginations toward the positive by using your will. Until you learn how to cast down corrupted imaginations, you cannot cultivate the positive ones. The devil wants to use your imagination to make mountains out of molehills to discourage. Devilish mountains are best built within a corrupted imagination. They only offer discouragement, fear, confusion, anger and defeat. The good news is that you can do something about them. You can take control of your thought life.

## OUT WITH THE TRASH

Imaginations make believers with mighty potential spiritually weak and emotionally immature. Some get carried away by their own imaginations. Relationships, for example, split because of vain imaginations.

Vain imaginations can be so serious that some even leave good churches because of imaginary offenses. Somebody imagined that somebody else thought something about them. Before they know it, they're giving life to corrupted thoughts, changing churches and abandoning life-long friends. They find themselves out of the plan of God and wondering what happened. Left unchecked this is the power of vain imaginations.

Every single time an imagination enters your life, you have to ask yourself if the thoughts line up with God's Word. If they don't, then you need to place them in a polyethylene trash bag for pickup. Don't be afraid to call a devil inspired imagination what it is. You need to say to yourself, "That's a corrupted imagination and I'm not walking in it." If you take one point away from this chapter, this is the one you need to take: When vain imaginations enter the spirit of your mind don't dwell on them, bind them up. Lingering on hollow thoughts and imaginations only empowers them.

Let's make this more personal. Let's say, for example, that you can't pay your bills. The devil will try to get into your emotions and torment you with thoughts that say, "They're going to take your car away from you, for example, or they're going to put a lien on your home, or they're going to file a lawsuit against you." Before you know it, you are tormented by an imagination, a mental picture of things that are not true.

Imaginations are suggestive and always rise against the knowledge of God that says, all of your needs shall be met. So what happens if you dwell on a corrupted imagination? You will be mentally troubled and prodded to act out the imagination. Do you see it? Imaginations are destroying lives, but you can stop every one of them by subjecting them to God's written Word. You can have the opposite of that vain imagination, which is exactly what the enemy is trying to steal from you.

## ACTION EXERCISE

Imagination is a good thing. As mentioned already. it is a gift from God given to you to "see all things as possible to him that believeth" (Mark 9:23). Before you can operate in that seeing gift, however, you need to discern corrupted thoughts and vain imaginations. You can do it. This week try writing them down and practice identifying every positive and negative thought, voice and imagination that enters your mind. The first step to winning the war, like Agatha Christie's fictional detective Miss Marple, will be your ability to rightly discern the thoughts that attack your soul.

In the next chapter, you will learn how to stop the whispers in your ear associated with vain thinking and imaginations.

## APERCU

With your spirit you connect to the unseen spirit world, with your body the natural world, and with your soul the magnificent world of imagination.

Your soul hosts your mind, will, emotion, imagination, reasoning and intellect. The warfare that attacks your mind operates within your soul, particularly your thought life and within your imagination.

Vain imaginations are those corrupted negative images and possibilities that form within the spirit of your mind when you linger on negative thoughts.

Imagination produces emotion.

Imaginations are pictures within your mind of thoughts, events or conversations that are only in the unseen world within you.

When you form, in the spirit of your mind, a picture or an image of something that *might* happen and act on that image you give life to it.

Acting on an imagination moves your life in that direction.

You can direct your imaginations toward the positive by using your will.

*Chapter 2*

# WHISPERS IN YOUR EARS

*Have you felt like you just wanted to give up and quit? Monday morning has come and you just want to ignore the alarm clock and pull the covers over your head. One of the surest signs of spiritual attack against the mind is the feeling that you want to throw up your hands and surrender.*

Spiritual battles are not fought with fleshly ordinance. Scripture declares, "For though we walk in the flesh; we do not war after the flesh" (2 Corinthians 10:3). Spiritual warfare isn't mysterious or mystical. It's using the Word of God and your delegated authority to oppose demonic opposition against you.

The Holy Spirit is still giving us understanding of the ghostly powers that battle against us in the unseen realm. Scripture says, "We wrestle not against flesh and blood" (Ephesians 6). The Apostle Paul makes it clear that we are in a spiritual war and declares that, "The weapons of our warfare are not carnal but mighty through God to the pulling down of strongholds."

Before we attack principalities and powers. let's learn how to pull down the warring thoughts and imaginations that rise within us. Paul exhorted us, "Casting down imaginations." An imagination is an image, a picture formed in the spirit of your mind of something unseen. Something that exists only in the imagination is not real unless you give life to it. Have you experienced an imagination today? What did you do with it? Did you cast it down and move ahead or have tea and biscuits on white clothed tables?

Spiritual warfare against the mind releases fear, confusion, despair and offense. Scripture says such things do not come from God,

"For God hath not given us the spirit of fear, but of power, and of love and of a sound mind." (2 Timothy 1:7)

## THE GREY HAZE

Let's start with confusion. Corrupted imaginations can affect sound judgment and inject confusion into your life. Left unrestrained they will release uncertainty and cause difficulty with solving problems, staying attentive and remaining focused. Confusion is like a grey haze that dares you to enter. Mental murk is the symptom of a weapon that clouds the truth. That's why its source needs to be justly observed. Sometimes lack of rest, health or disinformation affects your ability to solve problems or clear your thoughts. At other times, it's the result of spiritual attacks, warfare within your mind, that produces mixed-up thinking.

When the haze assaults remember this: "God is not the author of confusion but of peace" (1 Corinthians 14:33). Often confusion is a spiritual attack against your mind that has little or nothing to do with the general circumstances surrounding you. When attacked by confusion, plead the blood of Jesus over your mind and watch the cloudiness disappear like the morning fog at sunrise.

# LONELY WINTERS

Sad news can release despair. Yet dismay from spiritual warfare usually has nothing to do with a winter's tale. Have you felt like you just wanted to give up and quit? Monday morning has come and you just want to turn off the alarm and pull the covers over your head. One of the surest signs of spiritual attack against the mind is the feeling that you want to throw up your hands and surrender. Despair feels like a lonely winter. It is the capricious notion that everything is wrong and nothing will turn out well. It is an attack against hope.

Scripture says, "Now faith is the substance of things hoped for the evidence of things not seen" (Hebrews 11:1). Notice that faith activates hope that resides in the unseen realm within. You have probably heard much about the importance of faith, but faith activates hope. Hope is the stuff that dreams are made of. That's why the spirit of this world attacks it so. If the enemy can destroy your hope, he can disarm your faith. Those times when you feel like quitting and the whole world is against you are sure signs that victory is right at the door. Pick up your double-edged sword and slay that feeling.

## PICTURED WITCHERY

Confusion can also be the result of witchcraft that whispers in your ear. Witchcraft is a spiritual force that battles against the spirit of your mind. Ungodly imaginations, for example, can have you entertaining works of the flesh and take you right out of the Spirit.

Some people are like the lone Joshua trees found in Southern California's Mojave Desert. They are surrounded by desert and void of the refreshing waters of the Holy Spirit. Those who live according to their own hearts walk in spiritual parchedness. Scripture describes them as those that "Have forsaken my law which I set before them and have not obeyed my voice neither walked therein but have walked after the imagination of their own heart and after Baalim, which their fathers taught them" (Jeremiah 9:13-14). Baalim was a darkened prophet that ministered in divination and witchcraft because of a covetous heart. He sold out God's chosen for "the rewards of divination," power, prestige and money (Numbers 22:7).

> One of the surest signs of spiritual attack against the mind is the feeling that you want to throw up your hands and surrender.

Thoughts that take you out of the Spirit are evidence of the spiritual war against your mind. Beware the fate of the foolish Galatians. Some thoughts are works of witchcraft within your imagination. Bewitching imaginations that lead you away from God's principles and precepts into the flesh need to be bound and cast down (Galatians 3:1-3).

Witchcraft works best inside one's imagination. Enchanted images are simply focal points the prince of the power of the air uses to attempt to steal Christ's abundant life within you. Scripture describes witchcraft as a work of the flesh.

> "But if you be led of the Spirit you are not under the law. Now the works of the flesh are manifest, which are these: adultery, fornication, uncleanness, lasciviousness, idolatry, *witchcraft*, hatred, variance, emulations, wrath, strife, seditions and heresies." (Galatians 5:18-20)

Witchcraft is a work of the flesh because people have the power to cast down orphic imaginations or to entertain them and walk them out. Beware the ritual of pictured witchery. You give life to an imagination by speaking it. Scripture declares that "life and death are in the power of the tongue." You have to be careful what you speak because the world of the spirit doesn't operate on what you mean, it operates on what you say (Mark 11:23). When you speak the imaginations that attack your mind, you prophesy over your life. So be cautious with your words because speaking vain imaginations, an activity of your flesh, is a form of witchcraft according to the Scripture you just read.

Others may have witchy thoughts about you and speak them over you. When they do, they give life to them and pass the assignment on. Now you have to deal with those spoken words. Not only was the imagination working within their imagination leading to wrong conclusions but now they've released the assignment of that imagination against your life; when they do, it releases confusion, a form of witchcraft. If this happens to you, don't receive it. Don't think about it. Don't agree with it. Don't repeat it. Bind it up and cast it down. Period.

Someone may say, for example, "I was thinking about you last night and recommend that you double lock your doors tonight because I just feel danger in the air." Or they may talk about how you're going to be sick and so on. Don't give life to other people's fleshly munitions.

When spoken, vain imaginations release demonic assignments through fear. If someone releases fear at you through one of their imaginations, again, bind it up. You can declare God's truth over your life by saying, "No weapon formed against me can prosper in Jesus' name!" Remember that warring against imaginations means that you chain every thought, every word and every imagination to the Word of God, even the gossiping words spoken by others. Some Christians are taken out by imaginations because they don't know how to campaign against them. Use God's Word in your life and take dominion over vain imaginations. Avoid other people's imaginations and don't try to combat thoughts with thoughts. Instead, use the Word of God and your spiritual authority to take them captive.

## BLIND PEOPLE CAN'T SEE

Enigmatic imaginations can lead to shadowed thinking and unsure living. Scripture says, "I pray that the eyes of your understanding be enlightened that you may know what is the hope of his calling and what the riches of the glory of his inheritance in the saints" (Ephesians 1:18). The *eyes* referred to in this Scripture are your spiritual eyes. With spiritual eyes, you receive understanding because God enlightens you by His Spirit. God desires that you might know the truth and not wonder what the truth is. Vain imaginations can dapple the truth of Christ, but the Holy Spirit wants you to know "the hope of His calling" and "the riches of His glory in the inheritance of the saints." Vain imaginations try to jail you in insecurity, fear and wondering. Learn how to battle against them by asking the Holy Spirit to lead and guide you into truth.

I went to a doctor with a friend once and the physician told him in no uncertain terms, "You're going to die." A report like that can release many fearful thoughts at you. I encouraged, "No, you're not going to die" because God's Word says, "With long life will I satisfy him and show him my salvation" (Psalm 91:16). See; you have to hit fearful imaginations with overwhelming scriptural force. This doctor was well trained in his profession, terrible in bed-side manner, and, like blind people, could not see.

We must attack facts with truth. Sometimes facts and truth conflict with each other. The fact might be that you are sick, but the truth is that "by His stripes you were healed" (1 Peter 2:24). The fact might be that you can't pay your rent, but the truth is, "My God shall provide all of my needs according to His riches in glory by Christ Jesus" (Philippians 4:19). Learn to use the spiritual weapons of the Word of God in your life and fight imaginations with the Word of God that worketh mightily within you. If the devil says that, "You'll never make it," use the Word against him and declare, "I can do all things through Christ who strengthens me." (Philippians 4:13)

## TITTLE-TATTLE

Your enemy is a crafty foe. He uses gossip to train you in releasing and entertaining offense. Gossip and demeaning imaginations journey together. Where you find one, you often find the other. Vexing imaginations can cause you to attack others by empowering you to gossip. I have experienced people entertaining imaginations that use the telephone to pass them on. Gossip is a sin. It is destructive and should not be engaged. Like witchcraft, it is a work of the flesh. If you don't like something someone's said or has done, then pray for them, but don't talk spitefully about them. We can't afford to harm God's children with our tongues.

Again, imagination is a gift. You should spend it wisely. So if you find yourself gossiping stop. When others are gabbing to you, remember that most gossip is not true anyway and there is always two different sides to every story. If they are chattering about someone today, you are next on the list tomorrow. Don't let your tongue contribute to the devil's attack against others.

Gossip transfers thoughts and imaginations to others. Be careful what words you take into your heart. Solomon's wisdom is beneficial,

> "Keep thy heart with all diligence; for out of it are the issues of life. Put away from thee a froward mouth and perverse lips put far from thee." (Proverbs 4:23-24)

I mention gossiping because the enemy uses it to train you to contemplate corrupted thoughts and pass them on to others. American humorist Josh Billings gives some sage advice,

"The best time for you to hold your tongue is the time your feel you must say something or bust."

Even white painted churches with tall steeples experience the spiritual warfare of vain imaginations. Scripture says, "Now I beseech you, brethren, mark them which cause divisions and offenses contrary to the doctrine which you have learned and avoid them" (Romans 16:17). Imaginations spoken against a church can keep leadership dealing with squabbles, divisions and contentions all the time. They keep them occupied with things that are not true. When imaginations attack, it makes people want to give up and quit. Those that advance these imaginations serve their own desires, agendas and, "by good words and fair speeches deceive the heart of simple people" (Romans 16:18). Avoid the gossipmongers within your church that attack leadership and dismantle the unity of the congregation and vision of the house. Eleanor Roosevelt said, "Great minds discuss ideas; average minds discuss events; small minds discuss people."

## ACTION EXERCISE

Confusion, despair and gossiping are common weapons of the enemy. They can come when others talk spitefully against you or during times of discouragement and rejection. How they come is not as important as knowing how to battle against them. Christ is not the author of confusion but the finisher of your faith. He never taught His disciples to battle with fleshly weapons but spiritual ones. Jesus said,

> "I give unto you power to tread on serpents and scorpions and over all the power of the enemy and nothing shall by any means hurt you." (Luke 10:19)

Use that authority today and attack every power of darkness, confusion, despair and offense that battles your soul.

The mind is not immune to the consequences of depraved reasoning. In the next chapter let's discover the process and find the escape.

## APERCU

Spiritual battles are not fought with fleshly ordinance.

Spiritual warfare is using the Word of God and your delegated authority to oppose demonic opposition against you.

Before we attack principalities and powers, let's learn how to pull down the warring thoughts and imaginations that rise within us.

Spiritual warfare against the mind releases fear, confusion, despair and offense.

One of the surest signs of spiritual attack against the mind is the feeling that you want to throw up your hands and quit.

If the enemy can destroy your hope, he can disarm your faith.

Witchcraft is a spiritual force that battles against the spirit of your mind.

Witchcraft works best inside one's imagination.

Witchcraft is a work of the flesh because people have the power to cast down orphic imaginations or to entertain them and walk them out.

Your enemy is a crafty foe. He uses gossip to train you in releasing and entertaining offense.

*Chapter 3*

# DEPRAVED REASONING

*Corrupted thoughts and imaginations will battle for dominion in your mind. They war against the positive, innovative and creative ideas, dreams and aspirations the Holy Spirit wants to impart.*

"The great successful men of the world have used their imaginations, they think ahead and create their mental picture, and then go to work materializing that picture in all its details, filling in here, adding a little there, altering this a bit and that bit, but steadily building, steadily building." So said author Robert Collier. This is the fruit of positive imaginations we all want to live in. Futile imaginations, however, must be cast down first.

The most challenging struggles of life are within. There was a time when the thoughts of man were evil continuously. Their minds were systematically corrupted by depraved reasoning. Scripture declares in the days of Noah,

> "And God saw that the wickedness of man was great in the earth and that every imagination of the thoughts of his heart was only evil continually." (Genesis 6:5)

This is evidence that hollow imaginations always turn toward evil that steals, kills and destroys.

> "And the Lord said, I will destroy man whom I have created from the face of the earth; both man and beast and the creeping thing and the fowls of the air;

for it repenteth me that I have made them." (Genesis 6:7)

Our Lord was grieved because these people did not cast down their tainted thoughts but rather chose to walk them out. This teaches how dangerous imaginations can be and the power of them to lead into sin.

## SIN-MARKED

There was another group of sin-marked people Jeremiah described as ones who entertained evil imaginations and slid backward instead of walking forward with God.

> "But this thing commanded I them, saying, Obey my voice and I will be your God, and ye shall be my people: and walk ye in all the ways that I have commanded you, that it may be well unto you. But they hearkened not, nor inclined their ear, but walked in the counsels and in the imagination

of their evil heart and went backward and not forward." (Jeremiah 7:23-24)

Today people do the same by following carnal thoughts and imaginations. Never in modern history have there been so many people tormented by corrupt imaginations. The Word declares, "Wisdom and knowledge shall be the stability of thy times" (Isaiah 33:6). If you don't submit your mind to the Word of God, you will never be stable. If you walk out evil imaginations in your carnal nature, you will be unsound in all of your ways and not able to live the life that God wants you to have. God does not want you to be unstable; He wants you well-grounded, sober-minded and righteous. You can do that by knowing His will, His ways and His Word. He does not want you, like those that Jeremiah describes, walking out corrupted imaginations. He wants you to walk in the light. The Bible says, "And you shall know the truth and the truth will make you free" (John 8:32).

## DEPRAVED MIND

Let's examine the voice of an imagination a little more closely now. Remember what God stated before the Deluge? He said man's imaginations were "always evil continually" and those images were leading them away from Him. In the New Testament, those with reprobate minds are the same.

> "And even as they did not like to retain God in their knowledge, God gave them over to a reprobate mind, to do those things which are not convenient; Being filled with all unrighteousness, fornication, wickedness, covetousness, maliciousness; full of envy, murder, debate, deceit, malignity; whisperers." (Romans 1:28-29)

A depraved mind is a corrupted mind. These people refused to submit to God's Word. Under the Old Covenant, He destroyed all mankind, save Noah and his family. In the New

Covenant, He turned them over to themselves. Scripture declares,

> "Be not deceived; God is not mocked: for whatsoever a man soweth that shall he also reap. For he that soweth to his flesh shall of the flesh reap corruption, but he that soweth to the Spirit shall of the Spirit reap life everlasting." (Galatians 6:7-8)

It is one thing to know the Word of God, but it's another to love, covet and hold fast to the Word of God. Even the devil and fallen angels know the Word of God, but that's not enough. He continues, "Even as they did not like to keep God in their knowledge, God gave them over to a corrupt mind."

These people's minds were defiled because they were slaves to their own evil imaginations. God turned them over to an evil mind because they chose to walk out their imaginations rather than submit them to God. Scripture declares that they were "filled with all unrighteousness." Sadly, these people entertained evil thoughts of fornication, wickedness and every evil thing. They even invented new forms of evil within their imaginations. Scripture declares these reprobates "know the judgment of God that they that commit such things are worthy of death, not only do the same but have pleasure in them that do them" (Romans 1:30). This is the destination of sullied thoughts and imaginations, spiritual death.

## SHROUDED AGENDAS

Spoiled imaginations are the birthing place of hidden agendas. If you have deceitful motives in your life or ministry, for example, you'll try to make others fit into your imaginary world. When you walk out concealed plans strife follows. Paul said, "For I delight in the law of God after the inward man" (Romans 7:22). The inward man is your born-again spirit. That is the real you. You are a spirit; you have a soul and you live in a body. The Apostle Paul said, "But I see another law in my members warring against the law of my mind." Paul discovered a spiritual war released within his imagination. Later he wrote, "The weapons of our warfare are not carnal but mighty through God to the pulling down of strongholds," the warfare against your mind.

As said already, the most important step toward freedom and winning the war against your mind is to recognize when a corrupted imagination approaches. Every strange thought that enters your mind needs to be examined. Consider its source before entertaining it. Vain imaginations are easy to recognize if you decide to pay closer attention to your thoughts because they are contrary to God's Word. They release fear, rejection and insecurity. Scripture says,

> "And be not conformed to this world: but be ye transformed by the renewing of your mind that you may prove what is that good, and acceptable, and perfect will of God." (Romans 12:2)

We will canvas this more later.

## POWER CHOICES

When vain imaginations attack, take them captive by relegating them to the Word of

God. You have to recognize what imaginations are: an attack on the purpose of God for your life. To win the war, you must use your power of choice and choose not to dwell on them. You must opt to hold them captive and make them obedient to Calvary's blood-stained cross.

> To understand motive is a great weapon against corrupted imaginations.

Choose to declare this over your life right now, "I'm going to make every imagination and every thought obedient to Christ's Word that I might test what is that good and acceptable and perfect will of God." Yes, you will have to "fight the good fight of faith" against your mind, but you *can* win every time. Make the right choice today.

Scripture teaches us to act like born-again believers, not unbelievers.

> "This I say therefore and testify in the Lord that you henceforth walk not as other Gentiles walk in the vanity of their mind." (Ephesians 4:17)

Unbelievers walk in the emptiness of their minds. That's the kingdom of unproductive and corrupted imaginations. You, however, are not like unbelievers that are bound with hollow thoughts and corrupted vision. You are free and can choose to renew your mind with truth.

Vain imaginations darken spiritual reason within your mind. Can you see that? What understanding should you walk in? The answer is Scripture and verse Gospel truth. When God speaks to you, He speaks to you Spirit to spirit, not Spirit to mind. When the devil speaks to you, he speaks to your spirit, to your emotions or through the spirit of imagination. That's how the voice of the enemy attacks. He did that with Eve in the Garden of Eden and he'll do the same with you. God, however, metes with knowing, not wondering. If you're wondering then, you are entertaining an imagination. You have to know the things of God by the witness of the Spirit of God and the written Word of God. These two, Spirit and Word always agree. When the Spirit of God speaks to you, you're never going to wonder what God's doing. You're going to *know* what He is doing.

The god of this world wants you to wonder so he can get you to host vain imaginations. If you do, faithless questions, doubt and fear torments. You may think you don't fit and even begin to lose your identity. Imaginations like spattered nail polish can stain your spiritual understanding while alienating you from the life that's in Christ Jesus.

Imaginations attempt to separate you from the love and life of Christ. Jesus said, "I've come that you might have life and have it more abundantly." If you're living out vain imaginations, however, you will be disaffected from Christ's truth because, the "what-ifs" that imaginations release set you on the wrong track with your life. Vain imaginations that are not cast down are dangerous. Avoid them at all cost. Don't allow them to steal your destiny. Take them prisoner with the Word of God and cast them down when they attack.

## SPIRITUAL STABILITY

Peter said some interesting things about the mind. He said, "Wherefore gird up the loins of your mind, be sober, and hope to the end for the grace that is to be brought unto you at the revelation of Jesus Christ" (1 Peter 1:13). He's talking about imagination and mental stability. If you're controlled by corrupted imaginations, you're not stable. You're an unstable person, a spiritual schizophrenic that needs help. Notice, too, Peter used the terminology loins. The "loins of your mind" represent the reproductive region, the birthing place of great achievements. The only way to gird up the loins of your mind is through submission to God. Scripture says,

"Submit yourself to God, resist the devil and he will flee." (James 4:7)

Let's examine what Jesus said about imaginations. This is a familiar verse, but you may not have thought about it regarding the realm of imaginations. Jesus said, "Thou shall love the Lord thy God with all thy heart, with all thy soul and with all thy mind (imagination)" (Matthew 22:37). The word *mind* includes the imagination or the spirit of your mind (Ephesians 4:23). This is the first and greatest commandment. Jesus taught you not to be ruled by vain imaginations but rather to love the Lord with everything that's in you, including your imagination.

How many of us lack wisdom from time to time? Scripture offers the solution:

> "Let him ask of God that giveth to all men liberally and upbraideth not; and it shall be given him, but let him ask in faith not wavering, for he who wavers is like a wave of the sea driven with the wind and tossed." (James 1:5-6)

"How can you vacillate in your heart," you ask? By listening to the Word of God one day and lingering on corrupted imaginations the next, you waver like the bride that can't make up her mind to wear white or ivory. When you do this, you are pulled by the Word of God over here and pulled by an imagination over there. Before you know it, you're tossed back and forth like the waves of the sea. The Word of God over here and an imagination over there. You get pulled back and forth. One day you're up and the next day you're down. One day you're excited and the next you're depressed. One day you feel great and the next day you feel terrible. Welcome to the land of instability produced by corrupted thoughts and imaginations.

## THINK ON THESE

Let's contrast corrupted imaginations with what the Word says you are to do with your mind. Paul writes his entire epistle to the Philippians and ends by saying, "Finally brethren." In other words, "I'm going to give you the reason I wrote to you. Are you ready for it?" He says,

> "Finally brothers, whatsoever things are true, whatsoever things are honest, whatsoever things are just, whatsoever things are pure, whatsoever things are lovely, whatsoever things are of a good report if there be any virtue, and if there be any praise think on these." (Philippians 4:8)

So if you're having an imagination or an untrue thought that is not honest, pure or lovely, then that thought is not what God wants you to ponder. We have to leave the realm of vain imaginations and entertain pure thoughts and intents from the mind of Christ. Let's be like Noah that "found grace in the eyes of the Lord" (Genesis 6:8).

## ACTION EXERCISE

Corrupted thoughts and imaginations will battle for dominion in your mind. They war against the positive, innovative and creative ideas, dreams and aspirations the Holy Spirit wants to impart. To avoid corruption examine the source of your thoughts against your motivation. To understand motive is a great weapon against corrupted imaginations. As you use the power to choose what you think stability and peace will give you that sense of identity and purpose you have been searching for.

In the next chapter, we learn about Satan's best warfare strategy.

## APERCU

The most challenging struggles of life are within.

Never in the modern history of the Church

have there been so many people tormented by corrupt imaginations.

A depraved mind is a corrupted mind. Every strange thought that enters your mind needs to be examined.

To win the war, you must use your power of choice and choose not to dwell on vain imaginations.

Vain imaginations darken spiritual reason within your mind.

These two, Spirit and Word always agree.

How can you waver in your heart? You falter by listening to the Word of God one day and lingering on corrupted imagination the next.

Corrupted thoughts and imaginations will battle for dominion in your mind.

*Chapter 4*

# SATAN'S BEST SPIRITUAL WARFARE STRATEGY

*Satan still uses the same strategies to attack mankind: the introduction of doubt and vain imaginations. He understands that God created you to image all things possible, even the forbidden.*

A tactic is a plan of action for attaining a particular goal. Satan has one goal, to steal, kill and destroy. Many Christians are interested in spiritual warfare strategies dealing with principalities and powers, territorial spirits and demons. There's nothing wrong with that, seeing as casting out demons is the first sign that should follow every believer. Scripture declares "And these signs will follow them that believe; in my name will they cast out devils" (Mark 16:17). But what about demonic thoughts and imaginations?

> It wasn't until the fall that sin entered the soul of man and altered his imaginations forever.

Spiritual warfare is simply binding and loosing in prayer and attacking on purpose spiritual strongholds of opposition and resistance against the Gospel of Christ in your life and in the territory God has called you to (Matthew 18:18-20). It is taking up, in prayer, the authority of the believer that Jesus gave His disciples (Luke 10:17). As I penned in my book *"Exposing Spiritual Witchcraft,"*

> "We are not wrestling against flesh and blood, but against supernatural powers

that cannot be seen with natural eyes. Many Christians, however, are void of spiritual discernment and are, in fact, carnal in their understanding of the spiritual activity around them."

This point is crucial: You are not wrestling with people, but with principalities, powers, rulers of the darkness of this world and spiritual wickedness in high places (Ephesians 6:12). Although understanding spiritual warfare in the unseen spirit world is important, most of your daily battles will be within your own mind and imagination. This is the first level of spiritual warfare.

## THE DEVIL'S FIRST MOVE

Satan understands spiritual warfare and uses man's own ignorance of his delegated spiritual authority and the fertile ground of man's unguarded imaginations to attack him. This is why it is important to renew your mind with the Word of God. Satan has no authority over you unless you remain ignorant of his tactic to use your imagination against you. In the beginning, man's imagination was pure and produced mighty exploits. Scripture declares that Adam was able to name every animal, bird and every living creature on the face of the earth.

> "And out of the ground Jehovah God formed every beast of the field and every bird of the heavens and brought them unto the man to see what he would call them; and whatsoever the man called every living creature, that was the name thereof." (Genesis 2.19)

It wasn't until the fall that sin entered the soul of man and altered his imagination forever. Let's examine Satan's tactics to defile man by corrupting his imagination. Before the fall. all thoughts and imaginations were centered on the mind of Elohiym, who says "all things possible to him that believeth." Man was only capable of good thoughts and positive imaginations. When Adam named God's creation. he never questioned his ability to believe it possible to do so. God created the creatures and Adam simply named them. It was that simple. But one day the power of sin altered man's imagination.

God created Adam and Eve and placed them in the Garden of Eden. Eden was the Kingdom of God on earth. It was man's place of habitation and dominion. In the garden, they were free to enjoy God's creation and govern according to their divine, God-created, God-like natures (2 Peter 1:4). In the garden were two trees, the tree of life and the tree of the knowledge of good and evil. Of all the trees they could partake, excepting the tree of the knowledge of good and evil. If they partook of it, the penalty was death (Genesis 2:17). Let's go back in time and watch the Serpent deceive God's greatest creation, our parents.

> "And the woman said unto the serpent, We may eat of the fruit of the trees of the garden: But of the fruit of the tree which *is* in the midst of the garden, God hath said, Ye shall not eat of it, neither shall ye touch it, lest ye die." (Genesis 3:2-3)

Eve knew the truth. She knew God forbade partaking fruit from the tree of the knowledge of good and evil, yet the Serpent challenged God's command. The Serpent answered, "You shall not surely die" (Genesis 3:4). Satan continued his attack against God's Word by creating opportunities to doubt. Everyone will experience times when the enemy questions God's Word in your life. It is how we respond to his challenge that controls the outcome. Eve didn't handle the challenge well. Satan, disguised as a serpent, offered his perverted opinion of God's decree.

> "For God doth know that in the day ye eat thereof, then your eyes shall be opened, and ye shall be as gods, knowing good and evil. And when the woman saw that the tree was good for food and that it was pleasant to the eyes, and a tree to be desired to make one wise, she took of the fruit thereof, and did eat, and gave also unto her husband with her and he did eat." (Genesis 3:5-6)

In this Scripture we learn the process of Eve's deception and Satan's tactics to use her imagination as a weapon against her: She doubted God's Word, gazed at the tree, took the fruit, ate and gave to her husband.

## CLEVER DECEPTIONS

The devil hasn't changed his strategy. The tactic that worked with Eve he will try with you by introducing doubt and focusing you on imaging the forbidden. Simply stated, Satan took advantage of Eve's imagination.

Eve did exactly as God had created her to do. She imagined the possibility. Like Eve, our imaginations are designed to image "all things possible," even wrong things. Eve took the bait by entertaining the possibility the tree would make her like God. The formation of that possibility was within her imagination. Just as God created her, she was using her imagination to create. It was, however, the wrong image. This is what happens in our lives, too. Eve pondered Satan's words within her seeing gift. To win the war against your life you must conquer the vain imaginations that attack your mind. When you receive a thought contrary to God's Word for your life, don't let it incubate within your imagination, bind it up and cast it down.

Here is the pattern that most people follow when a demonic thought is introduced: They look, take, eat and then give life to it by speaking it. Have you ever phoned someone only to get their answering machine? So you leave a message expecting to receive a return call. The return call never comes. While you were waiting the opportunity arose for imaginations to present all the reasons they might not have called you back. Your imagination runs wild and you get angry, only later to discover their cell phone was broken and they had to wait for it to be repaired.

Just like Eve, pondering a vain imagination is the same as eating the fruit on the forbidden

> Good people are not impulsive sinners. They don't just wake up one morning and say, "I'm going to destroy my life today."

tree. And if that is not bad enough you probably gave that imagination life by speaking it and passing it on to someone else.

## FALLING FROM THE TOP

Imagination and fantasy are connected. Let's look at this again because I want you to be able to see the root of spiritual warfare against your mind through imaginations. Imaginations are birthed in the soul. Your soul hosts your mind, will, imagination, emotion, reasoning and intellect.

> "And when the woman saw that the tree was good for food and that it was pleasant to the eyes, and a tree to be desired to make one wise, she took of the fruit thereof, and did eat, and gave also unto her husband with her; and he did eat." (Genesis 3:6)

The first thing Eve did was to see. The word *see* here means that she pondered the sight within her imagination. Just as God had created her to do, she began to imagine the possibility of the serpent's suggestion.

Sin is always conceived within the imagination of man. Good people are not impulsive sinners. They don't just wake up one morning and say, "I'm going to destroy my life today."

Elliott Spitzer resigned as governor of New York after being caught using the services of a prostitute. He attended Princeton University for his undergraduate studies and Harvard University for law school. He was a successful lawyer and happily married to a beautiful wife. Together they had three children. I submit to you that he didn't sin impulsively. More likely he was taken captive to sin because he continued to incubate lust within his imagination. Satan doesn't mind waiting for you to fall. He'll introduce an imagination and just wait to see what you will do.

Imaginations need to be cast down. Take note of this. It is one thing for you to have an evil thought it's another to entertain that thought within your imagination. Be careful of lingering on ungodly imaginations. When you do, that gives them time to conceive.

## EATING POISONOUS FRUIT

Vain, lustful and carnal imaginations come from the tree of the knowledge of good and evil. They do not come from the tree of life. Again, in the Garden of Eden were two trees, the tree of life and the tree of the knowledge of good and evil. The tree of the knowledge of good and evil had two types of fruit, good and evil. Do you think Eve partook of the good fruit or the evil fruit? No one knows, but I think she picked the good fruit. You'd probably agree.

On the tree, there were two different types of fruit, the knowledge of good *and* the knowledge of evil. Although these were two different types of fruit, they were both connected to the same root. Some people believe that all good knowledge is passive but what tree is it coming from? We need to seek truth and not just knowledge. The Word of God is truth. Use it to discern the thoughts and motives in your heart (Hebrews 4:12).

Sin is always formed in the imagination of man. The serpent came to Eve and challenged God's Word in her life. That's what the devil will do to you, too. He will challenge God's Word in your life and then try to pull you into the realm of vain imaginations to mull over his words of doubt and unbelief. That is the way he attacks you.

Don't allow your mind to tap into the realm of imagination to conceive sin. Know the difference between godly thoughts and ungodly thoughts and treat them accordingly. Incubate the good ones and destroy the bad ones. A sign of spiritual maturity is the ability to know the source of your thoughts and imaginations.

Eve looked, she took, she ate and then she gave. That's the pattern. People look within their imaginations, they take, they eat and they give those imaginations life. It is one thing to have an imagination and another to speak one. When you speak an imagination, you give life to it. An imagination is just an imagination until you speak it out. Scripture says, "With the heart man believes and with the mouth confession is made…" (Romans 10:10). It also says that "life and death are in the power of the tongue" (Proverbs 18:21). When you speak those imaginations, you give life to them. Let's make sure we life the right ones.

## ACTION EXERCISE

The greatest spiritual battles you face are not against demons, principalities, powers and territorial spirits, but simple seeds of doubt, unbelief and fear released within your mind. Like Eve, God created you with a marvelous imagination. You get to choose what you do with it. With it, there are no limitations. You can use it to bring forth good or evil. Now you know Satan's best warfare strategy. Eve failed but with Christ, you will succeed.

In the next chapter, you will learn how to test for true prophetic imaginations.

## APERCU

A tactic is a plan of action for attaining a particular goal. Satan has one goal, to steal, kill and destroy.

Spiritual warfare is simply binding and loosing in prayer and attacking on purpose spiritual strongholds of opposition and resistance against the Gospel of Christ in your life and the territory you are called to (Matthew 18:18-20).

Satan understands spiritual warfare and uses man's own ignorance of his delegated spiritual authority and the fertile ground of man's unguarded imaginations to attack him.

The devil hasn't changed his strategy. The tactic that worked with Eve he will try with you by introducing doubt and focusing you on imagining the forbidden.

Sin is always conceived within the imagination of man. Good people are not impulsive sinners. They don't just wake up one morning and say, "I'm going to destroy my life today."

It is one thing for you to have an evil thought it's another to entertain that thought within your imagination.

Be careful of lingering on ungodly imaginations.
When you do, that gives them time to conceive.

*Chapter 5*

# SEEING LESSONS

*Imaginations, like all prophetic words, dreams and visions, need to be judged for source, accuracy, motive, truth, purpose, intent, and clear meaning.*

Imaginations can be prophetic. In the Old Testament prophets were called seers. Even though you may not be one of Christ's five-fold ascension gifts of apostles, prophets, evangelists, pastors or teachers, through imagination all of us have the ability to see the unseen. We are all prophetic people.

Imaginations, like all prophetic words, dreams and visions, need to be judged for source, accuracy, motive, truth, purpose, intent, and clear meaning. God spoke to Ezekiel about the danger of vain imaginations.

> "And her prophets have daubed them with untempered mortar, seeing vanity and divining lies unto them, saying, Thus saith the Lord God when the Lord hath not spoken." (Ezekiel 22:28).

From this verse we learn how vain imaginations can pass as prophecy. Some also prophesy today when the Lord has not spoken. God told Ezekiel they spoke from corrupted imaginations and not by His Spirit. These seers – notice God did not call them false prophets – used untempered mortar, seeing vanity, divining lies and telling people their visions were from God when they weren't.

Plasterers call stucco mortar mix. Stucco is cement, lime, sand and water. Before plastered (daubed) on a masonry wall they mix the ingredients with water. As the mortar begins to harden the plasterer may need to temper the stucco by adding more water while mixing to make the mortar more pliable. If he doesn't add water and mix again the stucco will become impossible to apply.

God said these seers used untempered imaginations to prophesy. They were not mixed in the water of the Word. God told Ezekiel they were useless images that did not come from Him but within them. Prophets had to guard themselves, too, from the dangers of imaginations. Like the prophets of old, the source of all imaginations must be discerned.

> Imaginations, like all prophetic words, dreams and visions, need to be judged for source, accuracy, motive, truth, purpose, intent, and clear meaning.

## DANGEROUS RENDEZVOUS

These seers were prophesying from pictures within their own hearts. Like Eve, they saw, ate and passed their imaginations to others. God taught Jeremiah the same lesson. False prophecy and vain imaginations come out of the heart of man and lead people astray.

> "Thus saith the Lord of hosts, Hearken not unto the words of the prophets that prophesy unto you: they make you vain: they speak a vision of their own heart and not out of the mouth of the Lord." (Jeremiah 23:16)

All imaginations are prophetic and every one should be judged. These prophets didn't judge theirs, but you will. Spoken, imaginations become words that prophesy life or death. The Bible tells us,

> "Death and life are in the power of the tongue and they that love it shall eat the fruit thereof." (Proverbs 18:21)

Vain prophetic imaginations can lead you astray. They can be a dangerous rendezvous that unlocks trouble and every evil thing. Not only should you judge your own imaginations you should judge those spoken by others. God told Jeremiah not to listen to the prophets around him without examining carefully what they said. He told Jeremiah there were men prophesying the images within their own hearts and not from His Spirit.

God also warned Isaiah not to trust in the vain imaginations of others. He said,

> "None calleth for justice nor any pleadeth for truth: they trust in vanity and speak lies; they conceive mischief and bring forth iniquity." (Isaiah 59:4)

Vain imaginations, empty visions, are misleading. God taught Isaiah not to trust in them because they give birth to nothing but error. If God taught Ezekiel, Jeremiah and Isaiah about the possibility of vain imaginations then we, too, should learn from His instruction.

The English philosopher Sir Francis Bacon coined the phrase,

> "Be true to thyself."

We need to be honest with ourselves, especially when it comes to imaginations within. Information, especially vain prophetic imaginations, can be deceptive, misleading and destructive. The only way to discover truth is by testing your imaginations with the Word of God. What we need is seeing lessons.

Again, all imaginations, like prophecy, should be tested for accuracy. Scripture declares,

> "Beloved, believe not every spirit, but try the spirits whether they are of God: because many false prophets are gone out into the world." (1 John 4:1)

The word *try* means to put to the test for biblical truth. To win the war against our minds, we must put to test every thought, dream, prophecy, vision and imagination.

Here are 12 ways for judging prophecy. Like prophecy, you can use this guide to judge prophetic imaginations.

# 12 KEYS FOR JUDGING PROPHECY

## 1. Does the prophetic message violate the written Word of God?

The Holy Spirit will never violate, in word, deed or spirit, the written Word of God. Therefore, when testing for truth does the prophecy agree with the letter *and* the spirit of Scripture?

## 2. Does the prophetic message give glory to Christ?

Speaking of the ministry of the Holy Spirit, Jesus said, "He shall glorify Me, for He shall take of Mine and shall disclose it to you" (John 16:14). The purpose of all prophecy should be "in all things God may be glorified through Jesus Christ" (1 Peter 4:11).

## 3. Is the prophetic word ambiguous?

Does the prophetic message mean anything? Scripture says, "The Spirit speaketh expressly" (1 Timothy 4:1). A true prophetic word has understandable meaning. Even though we "see through a glass darkly" God makes Himself understandable.

**4. Does the prophetic word lead you closer to Christ or toward idolatry?**

Idolatry is anything that you would esteem, value or place before Christ in your life. Scripture is clear. Even if a prophecy is presented with signs and wonders coming to pass, if it causes you to "go after other gods" it is not from the Lord.

> "If there arise among you a prophet, or a dreamer of dreams, and giveth thee a sign or a wonder and the sign or the wonder come to pass, whereof he spake unto thee, saying, Let us go after other gods, which thou hast not known, and let us serve them; Thou shalt not hearken unto the words of that prophet or that dreamer of dreams: for the Lord your God proveth you to know whether ye love the Lord your God with all your heart and with all your soul." (Deuteronomy 13:1-3)

**5. Do the prophecies produce liberty or bondage? Do they instill peace and confidence or fear, disillusion, and discouragement?**

Prophecy should set you free, not introduce concern, despair and dread. Scripture declares,

> "If the Son, therefore, shall make you free, ye shall be free indeed" (John 8:36).

**6. Does your spirit bear witness with the prophetic message?**

One should have an inner witness within your born-again spirit knowing the prophecy is accurate (1 John 2:20). Scripture teaches,

> "For as many as are led by the Spirit of God, they are the sons of God. For ye have not received the spirit of bondage again to fear; but ye have received the Spirit of adoption, whereby we cry, Abba, Father. The Spirit itself (himself) <u>beareth witness with our</u> spirit that we are the children of God." (Romans 8:14-16)

**7. Have you let trusted and mature leaders review the prophecy with you?**

Although you are ultimately responsible for what you believe you should also seek the counsel of reliable leaders. Scripture says, "Obey them that have the rule over you and submit yourselves: for they watch for your souls as they that must give account, that they may do it with joy and not with grief: for that is unprofitable for you" (Hebrews 13:17).

**8. Does the prophecy strengthen, encourage and comfort?**

All prophecy should bring confidence, encouragement and comfort. If it doesn't then it's not prophecy. The New Testament foundation for prophecy is edification, exhortation and comfort (1 Corinthians 14:3).

**9. Does the prophetic messenger live the Christian life?**

Jesus said, "Beware of false prophets, which come to you in sheep's clothing, but inwardly they are ravening wolves. Ye shall know them by their fruits. Do men gather grapes of thorns or figs of thistles? Even so every good tree bringeth forth good fruit; but a corrupt tree bringeth forth evil fruit. A good tree cannot bring forth evil fruit, neither can a corrupt tree bring forth good fruit. Every tree that bringeth not forth good fruit is hewn down and cast into the fire. Wherefore by their fruits ye shall know them" (Matthew 7:15-20). Ask yourself these questions as you judge prophecy: Is the prophetic messenger living in sin? If so, should I trust the prophecies of someone living in sin? Is the fruit of the Spirit obvious in the messenger's life? What prophetic track record does this person have? Is the messenger living in rebellion? What fruit is evident in this person's life and ministry?

**10. Does the prophecy come true?**

This Scripture teaches how to know if a prophetic word came from the Holy Spirit or not. "How shall we know the word which the Lord hath not spoken? When a prophet speaketh in the name of the Lord, if the thing follow not, nor come to pass, that is the thing which the Lord hath not spoken, but the prophet hath spoken it presumptuously (Hebrew *zadown* in spiritual pride and arrogance) thou shalt not be afraid of him" (Deuteronomy 18:21-22). The Hebrew word "presumptuously" is *zadown* meaning spiritual pride and "afraid" is *guwr* meaning sojourn. This verse could also be translated "the prophet hath spoken out of spiritual pride and thou shall not sojourn with him."

## 11. Does the prophecy exalt self, selfishness, humanism, and fame?

Prophecy is not self-centered. Jesus said, "If any man will come after me, let him deny himself, and take up his cross daily and follow me. For whosoever will save his life shall lose it, but whosoever will lose his life for my sake, the same shall save it. For what is a man advantaged if he gains the whole world and lose himself or be cast away?" (Luke 9:23-24). Prophecies that extol the prophetic presenter or the hearer are not biblical.

## 12. Does the prophecy equip you to establish and advance the Kingdom of Christ and His righteousness?

Scripture declares, "Seek ye first the kingdom of God and his righteousness and all these things shall be added unto you" (Matthew 6:33). "His righteousness" is His right causes. When Christ returns He will say to His faithful,

> "I was hungry and you gave me meat. I was thirsty, and you gave me drink. I was a stranger, and you took me in. Naked and you clothed me. I was sick and you visited me. I was in prison and you came unto me." (Matthew 25:35-36)

Don't let vain imaginations prophesy your future. To win the battles against your mind, you must judge every thought, dream, vision, imagination and prophetic word. If they violate the written Word of God, cast them down. Take control of prophetic imaginations today and use the Logos to do it.

> "All scripture is given by inspiration of God and is profitable for doctrine, for reproof, for correction, for instruction in righteousness: That the man of God may be perfect, thoroughly furnished unto all good works." (2 Timothy 3:16-17)

## ACTION EXERCISE

Prophecy is a work of the Holy Spirit. The Word says, "Covet to prophesy" (1 Corinthians 14:39). We must, however, heed the instruction of the Lord and put to test everyone. It's obvious that some prophetic utterance comes from the Holy Spirit while others find their source within the corrupted imaginations of men. Don't be afraid to judge prophetic words. It's your duty, and it's for your own protection.

In the next chapter, we will take a look at the dark side of unchecked imaginations.

## APERCU

Imaginations can be prophetic. In the Old Testament prophets were called Seers.

Even though we may not be one of Christ's five-fold ascension gifts of apostles, prophets, evangelists, pastors or teachers, through imagination all of us have the ability to see the unseen. We are all prophetic people.

Imaginations, like all prophetic words, dreams and visions need to be judged for source, accuracy, motive, truth, purpose, intent, and clear meaning.

All imaginations are prophetic and everyone should be judged.

Vain prophetic imaginations can lead you astray. Not only should you judge your own imaginations you should judge those spoken by others.

To win the war against your mind, you must put to test every thought, dream, prophecy, vision and imagination.

*Chapter 6*

# THE DARK GANDER

*Imaginations create reality, even evil reality. God gave you freedom to choose how you respond to every circumstance in life, every thought that attacks your mind and every bad report that contradicts God's plan.*

Imagination is the incubator of all creative ideas, thoughts and dreams. Before the fall, man's imagination was pure. In the beginning, Adam and Eve created in the image of God, were capable of seeing "all things possible" within their imaginations. After the fall, however, when corruption entered the imagination through sin, history teaches that man's imaginations decayed into wickedness. This Scripture bears repeating,

> "And God saw that the wickedness of man was great in the earth and that every imagination of the thoughts of his heart was only evil continually." (Genesis 6:5)

When Eve pondered Satan's introduction of doubt toward God's Word, the first corrupted imagination entered the earth. The corruption of Eve's imagination continued to degenerate and spread as she passed that imagination to Adam. Don't misunderstand me here. We're not letting Adam off the hook. He willfully rebelled against God, committed high treason and suffered the penalty of spiritual death for his actions. As time passed, Scripture teaches God was grieved,

"And it repented the Lord that he had made man on the earth and it grieved him at his heart." (Genesis 6:6)

That's how serious the power of sin working within the imagination became. What we learn is this: Sin released a dark side within the imagination of man.

## CARNAL IMAGINATION

Imaginations create reality, even evil reality. There are over 400,000 registered sex offenders in the United States. The pornography industry, fueled by carnal lust and sexual fantasy, is larger than the combined revenues of Microsoft, Google, Amazon, eBay, Yahoo and Apple. Driven by debased images this blackened smut is a $1 billion industry in North America alone. Engineered by wicked masterminds, pornography is the creation and distribution of sexually illicit images that have no literary or artistic value.

Through the contagion of erotica, Satan uses the imagination of man to sin against God, himself and society. Unrestrained sensuous imagination have a dark side that leads to wickedness, debauchery and destruction. The infamous serial killer Ted Bundy, murderer of 12-year old Kimberly Leach was interviewed by Dr. James Dobson before his execution in the Florida State electric chair on January 24, 1989. Bundy confessed to murdering 30 young girls and women. He grew up in a Christian home, went to church and had loving parents. He describes pornography as the genesis of his fall into the abyss. In the interview just hours before his electrocution, he tells of finding, as a 12- to 13-year-old boy, a pornographic magazine in the trash near his home. In time, he became more and more addicted to pornography, especially violent images of tortured women. When that no longer satisfied his lust, he fantasized of sexually assaulting and murdering women himself. He said,

> "The most damaging kind of pornography – and I'm talking from hard, real, personal experience – is that that involves violence and sexual violence. The wedding of those two

forces – as I know only too well – brings about behavior that is too terrible to describe."

In *"The Road to Xanadu"* Professor John Livingston Lowes wrote,

"Fantasy and imagination are not two powers at all but one."

Bundy brought life to his perverted sexual fantasies. Commenting on the dangers of pornography he said,

"I've lived in prison for a long time now, and I've met a lot of men who were motivated to commit violence. Without exception, every one of them was deeply involved in pornography – deeply consumed by the addiction. The FBI's own study on serial homicide shows that the most common interest among serial killers is pornographers."

Bundy is an example of the dark side of unfettered and incubated evil imaginations. He leaves us with a flagged warning, "There are those loose in their towns and communities, like me, whose dangerous impulses are being fueled, day in and day out, by violence in the media in its various forms – particularly sexualized violence."

The good news is that Christ gave you authority to bind and loose every thought and imagination. Refuse to let Satan introduce demonic imagery into your imagination. Bind every image and cast them down. You can choose how you respond. Bundy didn't, you can.

## RESPONSE ABILITY

Everyday we are bombarded by secular television reminding us that we are in a spiritual battle against our minds. There is much concern about the economy, jobs, and housing prices, mortgage foreclosures, declining morals, attacks against family values, wars and rumors of wars, sickness, disease, terrorism and natural disasters of all kinds. It seems like the perpetual hostilities against our minds offers many opportunites to leave the realm of faith in Christ and enter the quagmire of doubt, unbelief and worry.

Once again I am assisted by the Apostle Paul's statement: "Casting down imaginations and every high thing that exalts itself against the knowledge of God." I love the power to imagine "all things possible to him that believeth." Don't you? Frequently, however, we have to battle the negative thoughts that

> **When we think something often enough, we begin to believe it's true and our feelings match what we are thinking.**

war against our minds first. This brings me to the testimony of Viktor Frankl, a survivor of the Nazi prison camps. In his autobiography, "*Man's Search for Meaning,*" he pens an inspirational testimony of humanity's potential for greatness whatever the circumstances. He wrote,

> "Our generation is realistic, for we have come to know man as he really is. After all, man is that being who invented the gas chambers of Auschwitz; however, he is also that being who entered

those gas chambers upright, with the Lord's Prayer or the Shema Yisrael on his lips."

Frankl stated that no matter the mistreatment by his demonic oppressors, they could never take away his choice of how he responded to them.

## BUILDING STRONGHOLDS

Vain imaginations pondered will build damaging strongholds in your life. They war against your mind and keep you from walking in God's perfect plan and purpose. Remember the degenerate progression. First the enemy challenges God's Word in your life by introducing such things as doubt and unbelief. Next you have opportunity to gander the thought and image it or cast it down. Further, you have the ability to linger on that imagination and speak it out or take it captive to the Word of God and cast it down. See the progression? The ability to give freedom to your imaginations belongs entirely to you.

The result of habitual negative thoughts and imaginations can send you spiraling into a state of depression. When we think something often enough, we begin to believe it's true and our feelings match what we are thinking. To conquer depression psychiatrist Aaron T. Beck developed "cognitive therapy" in the 1960s to stop negative thoughts by replacing them with more positive ones. He believed that depression could be stopped before it ever started. The Apostle Paul developed the therapy long before Beck. He said,

> "Be careful (anxious) for nothing, but in every thing by prayer and supplication with thanksgiving let your requests be made known unto God. And the peace of God, which passeth all understanding, shall keep your hearts and minds through Christ Jesus. Finally, brethren, whatsoever things are true, whatsoever things are honest, whatsoever things are just, whatsoever things are pure, whatsoever things are lovely, whatsoever things are of good report; if there be any virtue,

and if there be any praise, think on these things. Those things, which ye have both learned, and received, and heard, and seen in me, do: and the God of peace shall be with you." (Philippians 4:6-9)

God gave you freedom to choose how you respond to every circumstance in life, every thought that attacks your mind and every bad report that contradicts God's plan. Like Frankl, you have complete control over your thought life. All of us have thoughts. They can be good or bad, but thoughts are only ingredients we use to make decisions. If your thoughts are carnal, then cast them down. If they are positive, feed them. Your imagination can only incubate what you linger on, good or bad.

You have control over your thought life and nobody can ever take away your freedom to choose how you respond to thoughts and imaginations. The Word teaches of a demon possessed man with an unclean spirit that lived in a cemetery. When he saw Jesus, he ran to Him, bowed and worshiped (Mark 5). If a legion of devils could not stop him from coming to Christ then no devil, demonic thought or evil imagination can stop you from the abundant life in Christ Jesus.

## ACTION EXERCISE

The world has always been filled with doubt, unbelief and evil goings-on. The good news is that you, the born-again believer, are no longer part of that kingdom. You can escape the dark side. Christ has redeemed you and given you great and precious promises. Take control of your life and choose to respond to every circumstance of life, thought and imagination according to the truth found in the Word of God.

In the next chapter, we'll review what Paul taught to avoid thinking like Gentiles.

## APERCU

In the beginning, Adam and Eve, created in the image of God, were capable of seeing "all things possible" within their imaginations. After the fall, however, when corruption entered the imagination through sin, history teaches that man's imaginations decayed into wickedness.

Sin released a dark side within the imagination of man.

Imaginations create reality, even evil reality.

Through the spread of pornography, Satan uses the imagination of man to sin against God, himself and society.

Unrestrained sensuous imaginations have a dark side that leads to wickedness, debauchery and destruction.

The result of habitual negative thoughts and imaginations can send you spiraling into a state of depression.

All of us have thoughts. They can be good or bad, but thoughts are only ingredients we use to make decisions.

If your thoughts are carnal, then cast them down. If they are positive, feed them.

Your imagination can only incubate what you linger on, good or bad.

*Chapter 7*

# DON'T THINK LIKE THAT

*How you think affects your life. Fallen man walking out of the vanity within his mind looks for ways to fulfill sensual, fleshly, lustful passions. When he finds those passions they pull on the carnal nature.*

God created your mind for thinking. Your mind is like a critically-thinking super computer designed to draw on information for the purpose of coming to a rightful determination. It will continually search out bits of data from life experience, prior knowledge, even assumptions, to extrapolate a conclusion. To extrapolate means to use information as the starting point to gain knowledge, draw inferences and make decisions about something unknown. There are thoughts that *suppose* something and are nothing more than random bits of information without merit, proof, witness, or substance. Thoughts like that have no real value and are unsystematic. The most dangerous thoughts, however, are those that lead to a particular, erroneous belief.

The source of thoughts, your thoughts, needs to be discerned. Are they real or imagined? Good or bad, right or wrong? Was Hamlet on to something when he echoed Montaigne, who said,

> "There is nothing either good or bad but thinking makes it so?"

Can your thoughts make things so? Do they deserve your attention? Should they be reflected on and acted out?

Only the mature understand the wisdom of parsed judgment until they can assemble all the necessary facts and come to a rightful conclusion. These champions of the Kingdom know how to think. Like precision timepieces that carry the unfaltering sounds of tick-tock, they examine each systematic movement of the big hand until finally clarity forms within their minds. Then and only then do they move the small hand forward and enter the next hour.

How you think affects your life. The Apostle Paul taught his students not to think like flawed Gentiles. The Gentiles were outside the covenant blessings of God until salvation. Paul used them as an example. He said that Christ's disciples should not walk like the Gentiles do, in the "vanity of their minds." Or, put in different words, they should not live in banned imaginations. "How does one walk in the vanity of their minds," you ask? By trying to live out vain imaginations. Paul said,

> "This I say, therefore, and testify in the Lord, that ye henceforth walk not as other gentiles walk, in the vanity of their mind; Having the understanding darkened, being alienated from the life of God through the ignorance that is

in them because of the blindness of their heart." (Ephesians 4:17-18)

Remember the meeting between Eve and the fallacious serpent in the Garden of Eden? As already said, she looked, she took, she ate, and she gave to her husband – and he also partook. This Scripture teaches the power of toying with deceptive words and imaginations. Fallen man walking out of the vanity within his mind looks for ways to fulfill sensual, fleshly, lustful passions. When he finds those passions they *pull* on the carnal nature.

## WHAT'S IN YOU?

Satan's activities are still the same today, thousands of years later. He looks through ancient eyes for something in you to work with. Something small, perhaps a seed, something hidden from the sunlight just under the surface, or something buried deep within. It could be pride, rejection or lust. It could be bitterness, unforgiveness, even the love of money. Again, he has nothing to web except what's already in you. Jesus said, "For the prince of this world cometh and hath nothing in me" (John 14:30). What about you? When that old dragon draws near can he find anything in you to anvil? To win the war against your mind, you must, "Keep your heart with all diligence for out of it are the issues of life" (Proverbs 4:23). Carnal thoughts and pondered vain imaginations give the enemy opportunity to attack you.

> Satan's activities are still the same today, thousands of years later. He looks through ancient eyes for something in you to work with.

Peter also wrote about the dangers of vain words, thoughts and imaginations.

> "For when they speak great swelling words of vanity, they allure through the lusts of the flesh, through much wantonness, those that were clean escaped from them who live in error. While they promise them liberty, they themselves are the servants of

corruption: for of whom a man is overcome of the same is he brought into bondage." (2 Peter 2:18-19)

Did you get that? Carnal passion, stirred by the lusts of the flesh and vanity within the mind is designed to overtake you and bring you to the timbered stocks. That's why Paul said to avoid the vanity within the mind. Vain thoughts are enticements toward further carnality and conceiving sin. Like walking in cold sunlight, they pull on the old man, that carnal nature that needs daily crucifixion. Is he dead in your life?

An evil imagination is a death wound formed in the soul that has its roots in the fallen corrupted nature of man. It is a different way of walking, outside your design. Like an addiction, vain imaginations can grab you and pull at your soul beckoning the reapers to come. Spoken greed, for example, draws on the blackened sinful nature of man. So, too, lust that pants for the forbidden. Lust is fabricated first within the imagination then onto the flesh looking for its harvest. When pondered it's like a narcotic to the most addicted of junkies.

What did Peter mean "they are servants of corruption?" Bondage! That's right; slavery trenched deep within their souls. Those taken captive through cultivated sinful imaginations become slaves fettered to their own carnality. Paul's warning "don't think like that" is significant. "How can one be overcome by an imagination," you query? As mentioned before, by brooding evil thoughts within the mind, imagining them and acting them out. That's what happened to Eve. She considered what the serpent said; she pondered the outcome, and she partook of the forbidden thereby giving birth to sin.

Futile imaginations obscure vision and corrupt judgment. Scripture says,

> "Having the understanding darkened, being alienated from the life of God through the ignorance that is in them, because of the blindness of their heart." (Ephesians 4:18)

Your understanding can only be darkened when you are carried away by carnal thoughts and hollow imaginations. You must avoid them at all cost because they separate you from the good life of Christ and blind spiritual understanding.

All of us must avoid carnal thoughts and vain imaginations and cast them down as they occur, even those that come from others. As you become skillful at "casting down every imagination and high thing that exalts itself against the Word of God" you will experience more peace and a greater focus toward purpose within your life.

It seems we have come full circle once again in our pursuit of winning the battles against the mind. The bottom line is the mind must be renewed. Some try to get the Holy Spirit to grapple with their minds. The problem with that is you must be involved in the process by making every effort to renew your mind yourself. Give the Holy Spirit something to work with. Make the effort by studying to "show yourself approved." The Greek philosopher Epictetus once said, "No great thing is created suddenly." So meditate on the Word daily. It will impart life, truth and grace for living into your soul.

## JAILING CONFUSION

Once again, God created your mind for thinking. To win the battles, however, you must *change the way* you think. If you continue to dwell on vain thoughts and imaginations, your spiritual savvy will be hindered and darkened. We're not talking about salvation here, but spiritual revelation and discernment you need on a daily basis. No Christian wants alienation from the life of Christ. On the contrary, he or she wants everything, He has provided. Jesus promised, "Those that hunger and thirst after righteousness shall be filled" (Matthew 5:6). "Maybe sometimes" you ask? No, all the time. Those that hunger and thirst shall be filled. You can make it. He will quench every thirst. You can win every battle, every time.

Spiritual discernment is often attacked by confusion. To sharpen spiritual understanding, the Apostle Paul teaches "put off the old man… which is corrupt according to deceitful lusts" (Ephesians 4:20-22). The old man is that old, fallen and carnal nature. If you put on that old carnal nature, however, it will cloud your spiritual eyes and affect your discernment. The old man, you understand, dwells in dark, corrupted thoughts, vanity within the mind, and produces considerable fear. Thomas Aquinas wrote in *"Kingship"* of a self-serving king. He described this king as a tyrant that suffered much from vain imaginations. He wrote,

> "Whence in the Book of Job it is said of the tyrant: 'The sound of dread is always in his ears and when there is peace (that is when there is no one to harm him), he always suspects treason.'" (Job 15:21)

This old king refused to renew his mind and the outcome was a life of mistrust, suspicion and fear. I'm sure he died old, lonely and unloved.

Satan attacks the mind of the unstable. An unstable person, like Aquinas' tyrant, is fickle, emotionally immature and marked by unpredictable behavior. The wavering believer is an easy target because pondering vain imaginations causes one to falter in faith. Scripture confirms,

"A double-minded man is unstable in all his ways." (James 1:8)

Vain imaginations, like a ship dangerously caught in the grips of a winter storm, will make you think on unhealthy things. They have you fighting imaginary battles in your mind while distracting you from the real battles in the spirit. Renewing the mind is serious. The decisive point is this: every believer that wants assurance that God *will* answer their prayers should slay double-mindedness. Scripture offers a warning to those that do not,

"Let not that man think he will receive anything from the Lord." (James 1:7)

What a startling verse! To avoid vacillating, you *must* fix your mind on Christ the "Author and Finisher of your faith." Make up your mind right now, stick with your decision and follow through.

William Clement Stone was an author of self-help books and wrote about the effects of negative and positive thoughts. He said,

> "There is little difference in people, but that little difference makes a big difference. The little difference is attitude. The big difference is whether it is positive or negative."

Stone was right. What you think affects your life. Thoughts are ingredients that create attitude. As we have discussed before, imagination is the incubator of thoughts. When you linger on thoughts or images, it gives them time to hatch. Once thoughts are incubated, you give them life by speaking them. Good thoughts and imaginations are wonderful. The evil ones, however, can destroy your life if you don't deal with them. You, however, now know what to do.

## ACTION EXERCISE

A certain sign of spiritual authority is the ability to recognize the source of every thought. If the thought is good, fine, if it's evil, cast it down immediately. Again, Paul said not to walk like marred Gentiles in the vanity of the mind. The enemy can only work with stuff that's in you. Don't give him anything to employ. Decide today to put off the old man like last year's winter fashion and live out of your new nature. You can do it. Start now.

Like Cervantes' gentleman knight Don Quixote, invisible opponents are waiting for you. In the next chapter, you will learn how to take them out.

## APERCU

To extrapolate means to use information as the starting point to draw inferences or conclusions about something unknown.

There are thoughts that *suppose* something and are nothing more than random bits of information without merit, proof, witness, or substance.

Satan's activities are still the same today, thousands of years later he looks through ancient eyes for something in you to work with.

Vain thoughts are enticements toward further carnality and conceiving sin. They pull on the old man, that carnal nature that needs daily crucifixion.

An imagination formed in the soul has its roots in the fallen corrupted nature of man.

Those taken captive through incubated imaginations become slaves fettered to their own carnality.

An unstable person, like Aquinas' tyrant, is fickle, emotionally immature and marked by unpredictable behavior.

What you think affects your life.

*Chapter 8*

# INVISIBLE OPPONENTS

*Perseverance is part of the human spirit. There is not a hero in history that escaped a measure of failure before success.*

You can't drive in neutral. You must think. Thinking is pondering facts that lead toward a belief and subsequent action. Thinking is good because it keeps you free from the negative powers of impulse, emotion, instinct and carnal appetite. English philosopher John

Locke taught that thoughts govern the mind of man. He said,

> "The ideas and images in men's minds are the invisible powers that constantly govern them, and to these, they all, universally, pay a ready submission. It is therefore of the highest concernment that great care should be taken of the understanding, to conduct it right in the search of knowledge and in the judgments it makes."[1]

Locke also taught how people can find themselves in error. The first are with those that seldom reason at all but only do what others tell them to do. The next are those that put a passionate desire above reason or the sound advice of others. The third are those that use reason but have bad information. All this means that what you think leads to governed actions.

Derek Prince writing in *"The Spirit-Filled Believer's Handbook"* teaches that the baptism in the Holy Spirit leads the believer into a new spiritual blessing but also into a realm of "spiritual conflict." Could this be happening to you?

- "The baptism in the Spirit does not merely lead into a realm of new spiritual blessing; it also leads into a realm of new spiritual conflict. As a logical consequence, increased power from God will always bring with it increased opposition from Satan. The Christian who makes sensible, scriptural use of the power received through the baptism in the Spirit will be in a position to meet and overcome the increased opposition of Satan. On the other hand, the Christian, who receives the baptism in the Spirit but neglects the other aspects of Christian duty will find himself in an exceedingly dangerous position. He will discover that the baptism in the Spirit has opened up his spiritual nature to entirely new forms of satanic attack or oppression, but he will be without the God-appointed means to discern the true nature of Satan's attack or to defend himself against it."

Could this be a reason for increased awareness of spiritual conflict within your mind? Prince thinks it's possible. Unlike Locke, who addressed the natural, Prince explores the spiritual.

"Quite often such a Christian will find his mind invaded by strange moods of doubt or fear or depression, or he will be exposed to moral or spiritual temptation which he never experienced before receiving the baptism in the Spirit. Unless he is forewarned and forearmed to meet these new forms of satanic attack, he may easily succumb to the wiles and onslaughts of the enemy and fall back to a lower spiritual level than he was on before he entered this new realm of conflict."[2]

You are reading this book because vain thoughts and imaginations have attacked your mind and you want to do something about it.

After reading this far, you have surely become "forearmed." Victory is yours. You can win the battles against your mind and experience the abundant life that Christ has called you to. You *can* have God thoughts that govern your life regularly.

Apostle Paul taught that you can win the war against the mind with powerful spiritual weapons. He said,

> "For though we walk in the flesh, we do not war after the flesh: For the weapons of our warfare are not carnal, but mighty through God to the pulling down of strong holds; Casting down imaginations and every high thing that exalteth itself against the knowledge of God and bringing into captivity every thought to the obedience of Christ and having in a readiness to revenge all disobedience when your obedience is fulfilled." (2 Corinthians 10:3-5)

By now you have learned much about renewing your mind. Let's finish this essay with a short list of other powerful weapons including knowledge of the Word of God that divides spirit and soul, perseverance, pleading the blood of Christ, praying in the Spirit and praising God.

## DIVIDING ASUNDER

As we continue to conquer vain thoughts and imaginations we understand that obedience to the Word of God is a given. We know that it is the power of the Word of God, believed, spoken, and acted on, that demolishes every demonic stronghold that crusades against our minds. The writer of the Book of Hebrews explained the Logos of God like this:

> "For the word of God is quick, and powerful, and sharper than any two-edged sword, piercing even to the dividing asunder of soul and spirit, and of the joints and marrow, and is a discerner of the thoughts and intents of the heart." (Hebrews 4:12)

This is one of my favorite verses in the Bible. Its truth unlocks the mystery of holy writ teaching that the Word of God is a "discerner of the thoughts and the intents of the heart," your heart. It examines every imagination for truth, motive and reality. Unlike any other book in history it teaches you what to think, when to think and how to think.

> A captive imagination has no freedom to express itself.

When an imagination enters your mind, for example, you can use the Word of God to rightly divide and examine it for truth and use. This makes it easy for you. All you have to do is simply let the Word of God judge the thoughts for you, rightly divide them and give you the truth needed to make right decisions with your life. If the thoughts are good, receive them. If not, reject them. It's that simple.

Imagination is a powerful tool that unlocks innovation and creates many wonderful things. Many years ago I learned that the freedom to imagine must first be fortified with chapter and verse Bible truth. Some imaginations are good.

You might imagine how to build a more fuel efficient car and that's a good thing. But your imagination, your life and the spirit of your mind needs to be fortified with truth. When that's done, dream on.

We have learned throughout this book that man's destiny is controlled by thoughts, imagination, experience, reasoning, intellect and God's Word. The choice is always yours to decide what you draw on to make decisions. Conquering wayward imaginations is something that you have to do every day. That is why it's so important that you understand how to deal with them.

Sometimes the question is asked, "How do we know if an imagination has been taken captive?" The answer is clear. *A captive imagination has no freedom to express itself.* It is dead. If it keeps coming up over and again, then you haven't yet won the war against it. Be encouraged and don't give up. Some battles take longer and are more profitable than others and require more fortitude.

# UNYIELDING DETERMINATION

Perseverance is part of the human spirit. There is not a hero in history that escaped a measure of failure before success. Charles J. Fox, supporter of anti-slavery and American independence wrote,

> "Show me a young man who has not succeeded at first and has then gone on and I will back that man to do better than those who succeeded at the first trial."

The Word declares of those that know their God they will be "strong and do exploits" (Daniel 11:32). Perseverance is a godly trait. Dr. Orison Marden, early 20th-century motivational author, agreed. He said,

> "Most men fail, not through lack of education or agreeable personal qualities, but from lack of dogged determination, from lack of dauntless will."

Scripture gives us the remedy for fatigue. "Let the weak say I am strong" (Joel 3:10). There is something in verbalizing what Christ said you can do. Through Christ you can make it, you can succeed. All of us are products of decisions, faith and determination. With Christ, you are more than a conqueror.

## PLEADING THE BLOOD

The blood of Jesus is another powerful weapon that overcomes evil thoughts and imaginations. There is a revelation about the blood of Jesus that is important for you to remember. It is this: the blood of Jesus speaks victory for you.

Plead the blood of Jesus "out loud" over your mind when you feel attacked. This will help you because the blood of Jesus speaks powerfully. Scripture confirms it saying, "By faith Abel offered unto God a more excellent sacrifice than Cain, by which he obtained witness that he was righteous. God testifying of his gifts and by, it he being dead yet speaketh" (Hebrews 11:4) And "Jesus, the mediator of the new covenant and to the blood of sprinkling that speaketh better things…" (Hebrews 12:24). Pleading the blood of Jesus puts on that important piece of God's armor, the "helmet of salvation" (Ephesians 6:17).

The blood of Jesus is active and alive. It forever speaks on your behalf. That's why the devil cannot handle hearing about it. The blood speaks redemption, deliverance and blessing for you and judgment for him.

Vain imaginations are no match for our spiritual weapons. Scripture declares, "And they overcame him by the blood of the Lamb and by the word of their testimony; and they loved not their lives unto the death" (Revelation 12:11). The Word of God spoken out of your mouth, in faith, is your testimony of power.

Your testimony is what Jesus has done for you. The word "overcame" means to get the better of, such as in a struggle or conflict. It means to prevail over opposition and temptation. Use it to conquer the world of vain imaginations in your life.

## EFFECTIVE PRAYER

One of the most misunderstood and often controversial spiritual weapons is praying in the spirit. That means praying in tongues with the unction of the Holy Ghost (Jude 20). Jesus said, "Out of your belly shall flow rivers of living water" (John 7:38). He is referring to your innermost being; that's from your spirit within. Paul taught that we do not know how to pray as we should, but the Spirit of God within us does (Romans 8:26). Praying in the spirit (tongues) is a potent weapon to stop the war against your mind. So when the onslaught of imaginations attack, open your mouth and speak in other tongues until you get the victory. Paul said,

> "For if I pray in an unknown tongue, my spirit prayeth, but my understanding is unfruitful. What is it then? I will pray with the spirit, and I will pray with the understanding also: I will sing with the spirit, and I will sing with the understanding also." (1 Corinthians 14:14-15)

## STOPPING YOUR NEMESIS

Praise is another weapon that stops the war against your mind. An avenger is someone that retaliates against you. Have you ever felt attacked by some unseen force after you stepped out in faith? If so, that was the Avenger. Satan, your nemesis, hates true obedience to Christ and will retaliate against your faithfulness by attacking your mind. When he does, use your mighty weapon of praise to shut him up.

Scripture declares, "Out of the mouth of babes and sucklings hast thou ordained strength (praise) because of thine enemies, that thou mightest still the enemy and the avenger" (Psalm 8:2). The word *strength* is the Greek word *oz* meaning mighty praise. Mighty praise stops the enemy every time. The word "Oz" also points to might, power and strong (loud) praise. Now you know why the devil attacks your fervor in praise and worship. Praise is a mighty weapon against his assignments. Praise exalts God and puts down the enemy. Go ahead, sing that melody. Put that audio on. Lift your voice and fill your life with praise. Worship belongs to you. Use it and "still the avenger."

## ACTION EXERCISE

Victory requires thought and time, effort and sacrifice. Throughout this book, you have learned how to recognize vain imaginations and to cast them down. Now you are ready to incubate positive thoughts and bring glory to your father that has called you out of darkness into His marvelous light. Go ahead. Use your imagination the way it was designed, to imagine "all things possible to him that believeth."

In the last chapter, we will move away from winning the war against passive thoughts and imaginations into the future where dreams come alive.

## APERCU

Thinking is pondering facts that lead you toward a belief and subsequently an action. Thinking is good because it keeps you free from the negative powers of impulse, emotion, instinct and carnal appetite.

As we continue to conquer vain imaginations we understand that obedience to the Word of God is a must. We know that it is the power of the Word of God, believed, spoken and acted on, that demolishes every demonic stronghold that wars against our minds.

Imagination is a powerful tool that unlocks innovation and creates many wonderful things.

We have learned throughout this book man's destiny is controlled by thoughts, imagination, experience, reasoning, intellect, and God's Word. The choice is always yours to decide what you draw on to make decisions.

A captive imagination has no freedom to express itself.

The blood of Jesus is active and alive. It forever speaks on your behalf.

Praying in the spirit (tongues) is a potent weapon to stop the war against your mind.

**Notes**

1. John Locke (1632-1704), *"Of the Conduct of the Understanding"*.
2. Derek Prince, *"The Spirit-Filled Believer's Handbook,"* © 1993 by Derek Prince Ministries International published by Charisma House.

*Chapter 9*

# WHERE DREAMS LIVE

*Imaginations can change the world, your world. In fact, the world and history have already experienced change through someone's imagination. From the car you drive to the home you live in, to the clothes you wear, all have experienced the fruit of the creative power of imagination.*

Did you know the Holy Spirit uses your imagination to prophesy your future? Jesus taught, "All things are possible to him that believeth" (Mark 9:23). Can you imagine that? Can you see yourself walking out the promises of God for your life? Can you see yourself living in victory? Making a difference with your life?

God created you with a unique ability to see prophetic possibilities. We call that seeing capacity imagination. Imaginations create images of your future, of possibilities and of a better tomorrow. They can be prophetic, direct and give hope. To understand prophetic imagination is to understand God's design for His sons and daughters.

> God created you a Spirit-led believer, not just a spirit-born believer.

God created you a Spirit-led believer, not just a spirit-born believer. Throughout this book, you have learned how to cast down vain thoughts and imaginations that war against your mind. Let's conclude now with some positive attributes of imagination taken from my book *"Prophetic Imaginations."*

As you harness the power of prophetic imagination, you can enter the realm of "all things possible" and change your life. Prophetic visionaries see life differently. As a believer, you have the mind of Christ and the ability to control your imaginations and to direct them in a positive way. You do that by writing the vision and making it plain so you can set goals for attainment. As a born-again believer, you have power over the imaginations in your heart.

Imaginations can change the world, your world. In fact, the world and history have already experienced change through someone's imagination. From the car you drive to the home you live in to the clothes you wear, all have experienced the fruit of the creative power of imagination. As said already, Scripture declares that you are "fearfully and wonderfully made" (Psalms 139:14). God created you with prophetic imagination, the divine ability to see the unseen.

## FINDING GENIUS

Every great achievement starts within the imagination of man. Jesus said, "All things are possible to him that believeth." What would it be like if you could experience that truth? What would you do with your life? Did you know that everything starts with a thought, dream, vision, imagination, or image of something hoped for? Every improvement in the world, for example, was the result of someone imagining something better.

God designed you with the power of prophetic imagination to use as a method for great achievement. Prophets like Samuel, Gad and Asaph, were seers in the Bible. In a sense, imagination makes us all seers. Through imagination ideas are formed, songs composed and inventions conceived. By imagination thoughts of "what if" are pondered? Prophetic imagination inspires one to act, to try something different or to dream of better things. Dr. Lester Sumrall in his book *"Imagination"* said,

> "In the birth of human imagination, we witness the genius of the Almighty."

After the fall of Adam and Eve, as learned earlier in this essay, sin entered the imagination. Instead of images of all good things possible, unremunerative imaginations entered the earth. The first murder was the result of Cain's evil imagination that fueled jealousy, anger and rage. Afterward, man's imagination was used for destruction, carnal lust and rebellion against God. It's a fundamental truth we have made clear throughout this material. Scripture says, "God saw that the wickedness of man was great in the earth and that every imagination of the thoughts of his heart was only evil continually" (Genesis 6:5). God missed nothing. He saw the power of man's imagination for both good and evil. "And the Lord said, 'Behold, the people is one and they have all one language and this they begin to do and now nothing will be restrained from them which they have imagined to do'" (Genesis 11:6). From this verse, we learn the power of human achievement through imagination remained.

## WITHOUT LIMITS

Prophetic imagination has no boundaries and is never hindered by a lack of education. With it, you can enter the past and the future. What a wonderful tool to manifest the Kingdom of God in your life. After the fall man did not lose his ability to use imagination. The imagination, however, became corrupted. It could now see both good and evil. The good news is you can cast down vain imaginations and redirect your imagination to think, create and bring forth God's purpose for your life.

All creativity and innovation comes through prophetic imagination. Think about this. All things visible were created first in the realm of the unseen, the prophetic imagination. God created you with the ability to dream and to do great things. He continues to have high expectations. He expects you to multiply, produce, increase, subdue and take dominion of this world (Genesis 1:27). Imagine that.

As a born-again believer, you are part of a royal priesthood, a priesthood of kings. Have you ever heard it said that Jesus is the King of kings and the Lord of lords? Who are these kings and rulers? The answer is you and me, born-again believers. God created you with the ability to change the world starting with your world. Nothing can stand in your way. Believe today and use your prophetic imagination to change your circumstances and order your life for Christ in a brand new way.

## PROPHETIC IMAGINATION

The power of prophetic imagination is part of your human design. You were created with the ability to be led by the Spirit of God in your inner man and created with the capacity to see all things possible within your redeemed imagination. Creation and the ability to bring forth is part of the nature of God, who created all things from an image He saw and brought into being. God created you spirit, soul and body. Scripture declares,

> "I pray God your whole spirit and soul and body be preserved blameless unto the coming of our Lord Jesus Christ."
> (1 Thessalonians 5:23)

Before you can unlock prophetic imaginations within, you need to understand your spirit design. As a born-again believer, you are a spirit; you have a soul and you live in a body. Your body is not you. Your body is only the house your spirit lives in. Before you were born again your spirit man was separated from the life of God; it was dead in trespasses and sin (Ephesians 2:1). But when you repented of your sins and asked Jesus to come into your heart your spirit man came alive. Like I said in the opening chapter of this book, you became a "new creature in Christ Jesus; old things are passed away behold all things are become new" (2 Corinthians 5:17). Now you have the ability to *see* God's Word working in your life. You can now image "all things possible to him that believeth." That's the power of prophetic imagination.

## DIAMONDS WITHIN

Scripture declares,

> "A good man out of the good treasure of the heart bringeth forth good things and an evil man out of the evil treasure bringeth forth evil things." (Matthew 12:35)

The Greek word for *treasure* is thesaurus. Twenty years ago the word thesaurus would not have impacted me as it does today. As a writer, I often use a thesaurus to help me. Writers use a thesaurus as a tool to aid them to be more concise and descriptive. A thesaurus is an index, a storehouse and a place for word processing. Used appropriately, it enables the skilled wordsmith to paint a full picture through the proper use of words. Jesus said that a good man has a good thesaurus or treasure. Your treasure is the repository of truth in your born-again spirit. It is the dwelling place of "all things possible," the prophetic imagination. It is the storehouse of your dreams, imaginations and the blueprint of your future.

A good man's treasure has tremendous value. Jesus said,

> "The Kingdom of heaven is like unto treasure hid in a field, the which when a man hath found he hideth and for joy thereof goeth and selleth all that he hath and buyeth that field." (Matthew 13:44)

Jesus taught His disciples the value of the Kingdom of God. As born-again believers we have access to the Kingdom of God through our born again spirits. The Kingdom of God is not a place "out there" somewhere on the other side of the planet Pluto. The Kingdom of heaven for the Christian is all around him or her in another realm Jesus called the Kingdom.

Jesus also said the "Kingdom of God is within you" (Luke 17:21). Today, many call the Kingdom of God the realm of the Spirit. In that Kingdom realm, there is abundance, peace and fullness of joy. Again, Jesus said, "The good man out of the good treasure (thesaurus) of the heart bringeth forth good things." Notice that treasure and heart live in the same location. Where you find one, you always find the other. Your treasure is the birthplace of dreams, imaginations, and all things hoped for. It is the repository of all the elements that make up your future. From the treasure of the heart, a good man will bring forth good things. Imagine the possibilities of all things possible to him that believeth.

## YOUR VIRTUAL WORLD

Through prophetic imagination, you can design your own virtual world. Gustav Klimt was a famous Austrian Art Nouveau painter. His painting *"Portrait of a Lady in Red"* sold at Christie's auction house for $4 million dollars in 2001. He said, "Anyone who wants to know something about me ought to look carefully at my pictures." God could surely say the same, "Anyone who wants to know more about Me should look at My pictures." His grandeur is seen from mountaintop to mountaintop and from shining sea to shining sea.

What about you? What pictures are you painting in your life? Many are dreaming about one life while living another. If you are unhappy with your life, there is a way to change your circumstances. I want to encourage you to dream again and envision yourself achieving something great. You can master plan your life by imagining something new and fresh, then setting sensible goals for attainment. I can't stress this enough, imagination without specific goals for achievement is vain fantasy. Go ahead, dream again. Scripture declares, "If God be for us, who can be against us?" Be specific and biblical with goal-setting by writing your prophetic imagination down, making it plain so you can run toward your destiny.

Prophetic imaginations create theories, what ifs, innovations and views of possibilities. They help you come up with new ways to solve problems and succeed in life and ministry. Prophetic imaginations create your own virtual world of ideas. In that world, you can simulate your environment, try new things and envision something better.

> The world is waiting for you to unlock the creative ability of your imagination.

Virtual worlds are used in classrooms around the world to educate. They simulate possibilities while encouraging student participation. The ever-explosive computer games, for example, take children into a place where they can save the world from invading aliens. In 1982, Steven Lisberger introduced a virtual world in the movie "Tron," a world where a video game designer is abducted by a computer. Lisberger got his inspiration for the movie after seeing video games for the first time. The movie's tag line was, "A world inside the computer where man has never been. Never before now." Just like Lisberger designed the virtual world of "Tron," you too can design your virtual world. Use the prophetic imagination that God gave you and frame your world out of unseen possibilities.

## BETWEEN IMAGINATION AND REALITY

In 1959, Rod Serling introduced the American television audience to serious science fiction. The narrative for his new television series was, "There is a fifth dimension beyond that which is known to man. It is a dimension as vast as space and as timeless as infinity. It is the middle ground between light and shadow, between science and superstition, and it lies between the pit of man's fears and the summit of his knowledge. This is the dimension of imagination. It is an area we call the 'Twilight Zone.'" That place Serling described was "the place between imagination and reality." The show was a major hit and contained 156 programs in the original series. Obviously, it unlocked possibilities to millions of viewers. How many engineers and scientists began to see the possibility of a better world? Serling introduced the realm of imagination as a powerful creative force.

## ACTION EXERCISE

Prophetic imagination provides unlimited possibilities to you. It is the igniter of tremendous ideas that can be built on, expanded and brought into fruition. Whatever you can believe, you can receive. Jesus said, "What things soever ye desire when ye pray, believe that ye receive them and ye shall have them" (Mark 11:24). If necessity is the mother of invention, then imagination is the father. There are new inventions waiting for someone to vista and unknown worlds to be conquered by those who dare to dream. The world is waiting for you to unlock the creative ability of your imagination.

With proper use, imagination causes you to transcend limitation and empowers you to change your realities. Get into agreement with the Holy Spirit. Christ said all things were possible to him that believeth, so use your faith and unlock your ability to see. Scripture declares, "Through faith we understand that the worlds were framed by the word of God so that things which are seen were not made of things which do appear" (Hebrews 11:3). If God can frame the world with things unseen, then you too can frame your world.

This has been an awesome journey together. I hope that you have had as much fun as me. You have discovered that imagination is your seeing gift, learned how to cast down whispers, examined Satan's best warfare strategy, stopped invisible opponents and finally have explored the place where dreams live. I think you're now ready to make a difference with your life. Go ahead. Enter your virtual world with confidence and use your imagination to "see all things as possible to him that believeth." Dare to dream.

## APERCU

God created you with a unique ability to see prophetic possibilities. We call that seeing capacity imagination.

God created you a Spirit-led believer, not just a spirit-born believer.

Prophetic imagination inspires one to act, to try something different or to dream of better things.

After the fall man did not lose his ability to use imagination, the imagination, however, became corrupted. It could now see both good and evil.

Prophetic imaginations create theories, what ifs, innovations and views of possibilities. They help us come up with new ways to solve problems and succeed in life and ministry. Prophetic imaginations create your own virtual world of ideas. In that world, you can simulate your environment, try new things and envision something better.

Your treasure is the repository of truth in your born-again spirit. It is the dwelling place of "all things possible," the prophetic imagination. It is the storehouse of your dreams, imaginations and the blueprint of your future.

With proper use, imagination causes you to transcend limitation and empowers you to change your realities. Get into agreement with the Holy Spirit. Christ said all things were possible to him that believeth, so use your faith and unlock your ability to see.

## LET'S PRAY

Father, I come to you in the precious name of your only begotten son Jesus. I have had a problem with vain imaginations and warfare against my mind but now understand that you have given me spiritual authority to bind every evil thought and cast them down. And right now Lord I thank you that the weapons of my warfare are not carnal but mighty through God to the pulling down of strongholds, casting

down vain imaginations, carnal thoughts and every evil image that rises against the knowledge of God in my life. I take every one captive right now to your guiding Word and submit my life to you a living testimony of your greatnesses toward those who believe. I plead the blood of Jesus over my mind knowing that the blood of Jesus speaks of life, peace and joy over me and judgment to the devil and every demonic thought that would battle against my mind. I put on the entire armor of God including the helmet of salvation all of which guard my heart and my mind in Christ Jesus. Thank you, Lord, that you have given me a redeemed imagination that can see all things possible to him that believeth. From this day forward I pledge my heart, mind and soul to be that salt and light that you have called me to be. Thank you for a pure heart, stable emotions and the ability to imagine your greatness. And by faith, I declare freedom from the battles against my mind. In Jesus' Name,
Amen.

# JCM JONAS CLARK MINISTRIES

## Biblical answers you've been searching for...

Topics written with you in mind including, apostolic and prophetic issues, deliverance, healing and Spirit-led living. Great for your library or a gift for pastors, teachers and students of the Word.

**SPIRIT OF RELIGION**
Discerning religious spirits and entering the Kingdom.

*ISBN 1-116885-18-4*

**IMAGINATIONS: Dare to Win the Battle Against Your Mind.** Practical proven strategies cast down evil thoughts and be free.

*ISBN 1-886885-26-5*

**EXPOSING SPIRITUAL WITCHCRAFT**
How to overcome curses, demons, witchcraft and controlling powers.

*ISBN 1-886885-00-1*

**LIFE AFTER REJECTION:** God's path to emotional healing. Start prospering over rejection and reclaim your life from fear.

*ISBN 1-886885-22-2*

**KINGDOM LIVING**
How to activate your spiritual authority
Discover dominion restoration and purpose in the Kingdom of God.

*ISBN 1-886885-21-4*

**EFFECTIVE MINISTRIES AND BELIEVERS**
Introducing the apostolic ministry and what it means to you.

*ISBN 1-886885-25-7*

**STANDOUT LEADERSHIP**
Secrets of making more money, achieving greater levels of success, and making a difference with your life.

*ISBN 1-621600-14-9*

**DESTINED FOR DOMINION**
Discover the Christian's dominion mandate to invade occupy and influence the world for Christ.

*ISBN 1-621600-08-4*

**ADVANCED APOSTOLIC STUDIES**
Transitioning every believer into apostolic ministry.

*ISBN 1-886885-17-6*

**COME OUT!**
Don't ignore demons. Get rid of them! Stop demons, curses and witchcraft today.

*ISBN 1-886885-10-0*

**EXTREME PROPHETIC STUDIES**
Learn how to run with the prophets.

*ISBN 1-886885-19-2*

# www.JonasClark features Books, MP3s, CDs, and KINGDOM LIVING TV.

g on to www.JonasClark.com for Internet specials
nd for FREE bonus offers or call 800.943.6490.

**Jonas Clark**
Hallandale Beach, FL

# Effective Ministries & Believers
*Introducing apostolic ministry and what it means to you.*

Christ's disciples have fought raging spiritual battles with Satan for centuries. Some failed, others experienced limited success, but there is another group, effective believers that discovered the secret to victorious living. This group was taught by apostles that Christ would "build His church and the gates of hell would not prevail against it."

ISBN 978-1-886885-25-7

In *Effective Ministries and Believers* :

- Get the most out of your calling.
- Make a difference with your life.
- Discover God's design for effective ministry.
- Discover restoration and reformation principles.
- Gain spiritual strength to reach the next level.
- Learn how to invade, occupy and influence.
- And much more!

**To order Effective Ministries and Believers, call 800.943.6490 or visit www.JonasClark.com**

# STOP Jezebel Now!

Revelation about the Jezebel spirit is one thing – practical ways to overcome this evil spirit is another. Find out what REALLY WORKS to stop the Jezebel spirit.

ISBN 1-886885-04-4

The Jezebel spirit wants to control your life – and then she wants to destroy it.

Jezebel is a warring, contending spirit that uses flattery and manipulation to create soul ties that she uses to control her victims… and she's targeting you.

Find out how to recognize this spirit's wicked operations, which include false prophecy, fear tactics, seduction and many other wiles.

This book will expose this controlling spirit for what it is with explicit details, intriguing personal testimonies and letters from believers who have battled this foe.

Don't tolerate Jezebel… Get equipped and gain victory over this spirit today!

# Visit www.JonasClark.com or call 800.943.6490

# Exposing Spiritual Witchcraft
## How to overcome curses, demons, witchcraft and controlling power.

ISBN 1-886885-00-1

Spiritual witchcraft is probably attacking you – whether or not you know it. Every believer needs to learn how to recognize the weapons of witchcraft and be equipped with practical strategies to overcome it.

Spiritual witchcraft is the power of Satan. Its weapons are emotional manipulation, spiritual and religious control, isolation, soul ties, fear, confusion, loss of personal identity, sickness, depression and prophetic divination. Those caught in the snare of this spirit struggle throughout their Christian lives to remain stable. In order to successfully battle spiritual witchcraft you must thoroughly understand your rights as children of God because this demonic force craves to enslave those who are ignorant to the truth.

"I fought this spirit from April to November and won. So can you!"
– Author, Jonas Clark

**To order Exposing Spiritual Witchcraft, log on to www.JonasClark.com or call 800.943.6490.**

# Kingdom Living
## Dominion, Authority, Purpose

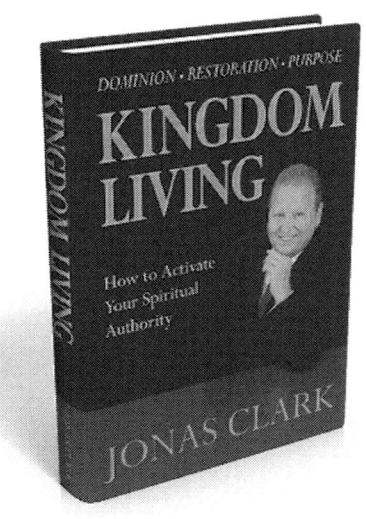

ISBN 978-1-886885-21-9
HardCover

**Are you experiencing Kingdom Living?**

Jonas shows you how to activate your kingship and live a life of purpose, authority and dominion that belongs to you in Christ.

***Kingdom Living*** offers practical insights into what Jesus meant when He said, "It is the Father's good pleasure to give unto you the Kingdom."

This book unlocks mysteries of the Kingdom for your life. When you read ***Kingdom Living*** you will discover how to tap into the power of the Kingdom of God in you and how to pray the way Jesus prayed.

***Kingdom Living*** equips you with action steps designed to help you experience what the Bible says about restoration, dominion, spiritual authority – and your role in the Kingdom of God.

To order Kingdom Living,
call 800.943.6490 or
visit www.JonasClark.com.

# Easy Read Pocket-sized Books

Jezebel & Prophetic Ministry • Entering Prophetic Ministry
How Witchcraft Spirits Attack • Seeing What Others Can't
Unlocking Prophetic Imaginations

Healing Rejection & Emotional Abuse • Overcoming Dark Imaginations
What To Do When You Feel Like Giving Up • Prophecy Without
Permission • The Weapons of Your Warfare

More Titles: Avoiding Foreign Spirits • How Prophets Fail •
Breaking Christian Witchcraft • Identifying Prophetic Spiritists • How Jezebel Hijacks Prophetic Ministry • Unlocking Your
Spiritual Authority • Prophetic Confrontation

## For more easy read Pocket-sized books visit www.JonasClark.com or call 800.943.6490.

Global Cause Network Champion Partnership
# JOIN THE REVOLUTION

"The Spirit of God told me to start a revolution by bringing apostolic identity to the Body of Christ. He told me there were thousands of people who were tired of dead tradition and lifeless religion and that we must break free from a one-man-only structure of ministry dependence and bless-me-only pre-programmed services into equipping, impacting, activating, and releasing every believer into ministry. That's when I launched the Global Cause Network (GCN), a network of believers, ministries and churches united together to build a platform for the apostolic voice." – Jonas Clark

Hook up with believers just like you.

Attend GCN - summits and receive impartation, activation, confirmation and release.

Get free powerful monthly reaching materials designed to equip you for ministry.

Go to the nations with us on an apostolic invasion team for hands-on ministry.

Enjoy 10% partner discounts on select products.

Become a GCN Champion Partner and together we can reach the Nations with the Gospel of Jesus Christ.

To learn more and join visit:
www.JonasClark.com
Or call: 800.943.6490

GLOBAL CAUSE NETWORK
27 West Hallandale Beach Blvd.
Hallandale Beach, FL 33009-5347

Apostle Jonas Clark
Founder, Global
Cause Network